Josiah Dwight Whitney

An Address on the Propriety of Continuing the State

Geological Survey of California

Josiah Dwight Whitney

An Address on the Propriety of Continuing the State Geological Survey of California

ISBN/EAN: 9783744691598

Printed in Europe, USA, Canada, Australia, Japan

Cover: Foto ©ninafisch / pixelio.de

More available books at **www.hansebooks.com**

AN ADDRESS

ON THE

PROPRIETY OF CONTINUING THE

State Geological Survey of California

DELIVERED BEFORE THE LEGISLATURE

At Sacramento, Thursday Evening,

January 30th, 1868:

To which are appended:

TWO LETTERS TO THE GOVERNOR RELATIVE TO THE PROGRESS OF THE GEOLOGICAL SURVEY
COMMUNICATED TO THE LEGISLATURES OF 1865-6 AND 1867-8 ; ALSO, THE REPORT
OF THE COMMISSIONERS TO MANAGE THE YOSEMITE VALLEY AND THE
MARIPOSA BIG TREE GROVE, FOR THE YEARS 1867-8.

By J. D. WHITNEY,

STATE GEOLOGIST.

SAN FRANCISCO:

TOWNE AND BACON.

1868.

ADDRESS.

Gentlemen of the Senate and Assembly :

For the fourth time I am summoned to appear before the honorable Legislature of the State of California to give an account of my stewardship ; and, embarrassed as I am between the desire of saying something which shall both interest and amuse, and that of crowding as much of instructive matter as possible into the allotted hour, I feel the necessity of asking your attention to what I have to say as a matter of business, even if I should not succeed in investing a somewhat dry subject with the graces of elocutionary display. There are 125,600 good reasons (almighty good ones to those who worship the almighty dollar) why I should be heard, since those figures represent the amount which the State has already expended on the Geological Survey, and if the money has been misspent, it is your duty to see that no more goes the same way. In inviting the State Geologist, therefore, to speak for himself, you have taken the shortest and most direct method of getting at the exact truth in this matter ; and that the truth should be got at, before decisive action is had, seems to me no more than is reasonable to ask. I believe that, without exception, whenever there has been any opposition to our work, it has come from those who have taken no pains to inform themselves as to its real nature, from those who have never set foot in our office to examine what was going on there, and who have thus been actuated by blind prejudice rather than by any real desire to economize ; for, not to put too fine a point upon it, the whole question of the continuance of the survey is simply a question of economy ; it is just this — does it pay, or does it not pay ? There is, I imagine, hardly a man in the State who would venture to oppose the continuance of the survey on any other ground than that of economy.

Not a whisper of opposition has ever been raised against the work, which has quietly and effectively been going on for the last twenty years on our coast, at an annual cost ten times greater than that of the Geological Survey, but at the expense of the United States, and the object of which is to give to this State, and all who need it, a map of the line along which old Ocean thunders against our rocky shores. No ; the money does not come directly out of our pockets, let the great work go on ; we see its value and approve its progress. But the Geological Survey—that is quite another thing : getting information *gratis*, and paying for the same, are two essentially different institutions.

A bill has been, or is to be, introduced, I am told, abolishing the State Geologist and consigning him to the tomb of the Capulets. This seems to me decidedly a work of supererogation, since that unfortunate officer is, to speak metaphorically, already in the last gasp of dissolution. If the Act is to be of any value it must be passed in a hurry, or you will be hanging a man who has just died of starvation. The train can be stopped just as well, and with less damage to the property of the State which is on board, by putting no more wood under the boiler and shutting off steam gradually, as by putting a rail on the track and thus throwing the engine off and smashing things generally.

At the time of commencing the survey, I had the honor of delivering my inaugural address before the Legislature, and in this I gave, in a highly condensed form, a history of the development of the mineral resources of the United States with special reference to what had been accomplished in this behalf by the different State Geological Surveys. Having glanced at the condition of the mining interests of this country, as compared with those of other parts of the world, I stated what the Act by which this survey was authorized called for, and laid out the work on which we were about to enter as well as could be done by one bringing with him a large amount of experience gathered in other regions, although but little acquainted, from personal observation, with the new field on which he was about to enter.

The next year, having the honor of addressing the Legislature without being especially called on by that body to select any particular subject, I endeavored to give some idea of the nature of geological inquiries, in their broadest and most generally attractive direction, and to awaken an interest in our work by setting forth some of the most interesting results at which geologists have arrived during the few years just past, and in various parts of the world, making my lecture a sort of spelling book and dictionary of our future reports ; but not letting go my hold on my audience until, as in duty bound, I had said a few words in regard to the advantages to be derived from a thorough prosecution of the work on which we had then fully entered.

Once more the State Geologist appeared in this place and addressed the Legislature, by request, on the question of the establishment of a State University in California, giving some of the results acquired by many years' experience as a pupil, resident graduate or professor in several institutions of learning of the highest rank, on both sides of the Atlantic, including Yale and Harvard Colleges, the School of Mines in Paris and the Universities of Giessen and Berlin.

On both these last occasions I endeavored to set forth in as clear a light as possible the relations of the survey to the cause of higher education in this State and on the Pacific Coast in general—a subject which is by no means exhausted, and on which I will ask permission, before closing, to add a few more last words, in view of the fact that the question of a State University is again before you for discussion, and in the hope that my ideas may be found not unworthy of being heeded.

On this solemn occasion, when the fate of the survey seems about to be decided, and I, perhaps, may be preaching its funeral sermon, if I were to search for a text on which to base my discourse, I do not know that I could find one better than that containing a malediction on the man who looks back after putting his hand to the plow ; for this text exactly expresses the sentiment which has actuated me in pushing this great work along against every obstacle — want of sympathy among the people, want of sufficient appropriations from the Legislature, want of sufficient knowledge on the part of many to understand the real extent and probable value of our results, but no want of misapprehension and misstatement of our motives and actions, or of abuse in the newspapers for not doing what we have done, and for doing that which we have not done. A constitutional antipathy on the part of its chief to looking back after having laid his hand on the plow is the one effective reason why this survey has not long since been wound up and its fossil remains left in the pigeon-hole, over which, in big black letters, the ominous word "Fizzle" stands, as representing a great undertaking abandoned for want of pluck and energy to see it through.

It has been repeatedly thrown in our teeth that we were trying to accomplish too much ; that our plans were too extensive, and that we were aiming at something it was beyond our power or that of the State to accomplish. Let us see : the Legislature ordered " An accurate and complete geological survey of this State, with proper maps and diagrams thereof, together with a full and scientific description of its rocks, fossils, soils and minerals, and of its botanical and zoölogical productions." I quote the exact language of the Act. Suppose, now, it had read thus : " The State Geologist shall make a hasty and inaccurate survey of the State, and furnish unreliable and worthless maps of the same, together with a popular and amusing account of his travels, and private reports to mining speculators, on the principle of the bigger the fee the more favorable the report." Does any one suppose that a scientific man, with a reputation and a conscience, could have been found to lend his name to such a ridiculous proposition ? And the scientific man who should make himself responsible for the statement that anything but a hasty and inaccurate, and consequently worthless, survey could be made without much time, labor and money, would be either a knave or a fool, or both.

The State Geologist is not responsible for the plan of the survey ; all he has sought to do was to carry out the arduous task set before him by the Legislature to the best of his ability, giving the best years of his life and his undivided energies to the work, with no other object in view than that of so executing it that it would be of permanent value to the State, and consequently a credit to himself.

What, then, is the object of the Geological Survey, and for what purpose has it been instituted? This question I will endeavor to answer, and I will then show, as far as possible, within the limitations imposed on me by time and place, how much progress has been made in it ; and finally, will give some reasons why, as I think, the work should be continued to completion, and that on the scale and with the plan on which it was started, and on which it has thus far been carried on.

The object of the Geological Survey may be succinctly stated in these words : " It is to give to the world, and especially to our own citizens, an encyclopædic statement of the natural resources and capabilities of the State." Its scope may, perhaps, be better comprehended if we consider what a private individual would do if he were to come into possession, by legacy or otherwise, of a vast estate of unexplored and unsurveyed territory, in regard to the value of which there were no certain data in existence. If unable to examine his newly acquired property himself, he would hire others to explore, survey and map it, to investigate its capabilities for settlement and its resources for sustaining a population, so that he might be able to cut it up and bring it into the market, or otherwise to make it available. This is just exactly what we are doing for the State; we map its surface, examine and describe its natural productions, whether animal, vegetable or mineral, and do, in a large way, as a unit, for the State and all the inhabitants in it, just what each individual would wish to have done, if he had intelligence enough to know what was for his own interest and the means to accomplish it, for his share of the great estate which belongs to the people and is to be made available for their benefit, individually and collectively.

The object of the Geological Survey being, as has been stated, to furnish an encyclopædia of the resources of the State, the mode in which this object was to be best accomplished, taking into view on the one hand the needs, and on the other the resources available, gradually shaped itself in the mind of the individual to whom the work was intrusted.

As thus developed, the survey is divided into three principal departments, each again with its subordinate divisions.

The three main divisions are : Geography, Geology, and Natural History. The first includes a topographical survey, the publication of maps, and also an account of the physical geography of the State. The second department includes general geology, economical geology, and palæontology. The third, botany and zoölogy. Thus, there are seven subdivisions of our work, each requiring one or more volumes for its complete illustration.

I will now proceed to state, as briefly as is consistent with intelligibility, what has been done under each of these heads, aiming to give some general idea of what we aspire to accomplish, and setting forth what remains to be done as the supplement of what has been done. At the foundation of our work lies the topographical survey, for without a map of the State we should be as much at a loss to describe its resources, as a painter would be in working without a canvas on which to embody his conceptions. It is not necessary, and would not be even before the most illiterate audience, to enlarge on the necessity and importance of geographical maps to every country ; as well might I undertake to demonstrate the desirability of putting up the frame of a house before putting on the clapboards and shingles. The exact stage of civilization of every country or State can at once be inferred from the character of its maps.

But a complete and accurate survey and map is necessarily a work of much time and labor. To give an idea of what has been expended in this way in other parts of the world, I will state a few facts gathered from the United States Coast Survey Report for 1858.

The total area of the United Kingdom of Great Britain and Ireland is about 120,000 square miles, or 40,000 less than that of California. The entire cost of the topographical surveys of that country had been, up to 1854, $12,000,000. And to complete the work, $20,000,000 more was required; 3,500 persons were engaged on the survey at one time. This is exclusive of what was being spent at the same time on the geological and hydrographical surveys.

The survey of France — an empire about one-fifth larger than our State—was commenced in 1818, on an estimate of thirty years for the time required to complete it and an expense of $20,000,000; 2,500 men, besides laborers, have been employed in the work.

Massachusetts, with an area only one-twentieth that of California, spent more on her geographical map than our whole survey has cost, and that more than thirty years ago.

It may be said, however, what is the use of parading these figures, which seem to demonstrate that the possession of a good map is something that we cannot aspire to? To this, I reply, in the first place, that we are doing this work on a very limited scale, as regards expenditure, and that we shall accomplish a great deal with a comparatively small amount of money; next, that if it is not done by the State it will be attempted to be done by individuals, and the result will be that no good map will ever be obtained; while, in reality, a much greater expenditure of money will be made. Private parties will be continually getting out new maps, each one of which will be a little more of an approximation to the truth, but at the best extremely defective; while the public will be continually buying these maps as they appear, rejecting the old ones already on hand, in the vain hope that each new one will be sufficient for their needs—a system which will be equivalent to laying the people of the State under a perpetual tax for the benefit of a few map makers, who work without ever having any prospect of attaining satisfactory results. Those who have not examined into the matter have little idea how large sums are spent in this way in the State. I consider myself safe in stating, that an amount greater than the entire cost of the survey has been paid out, during the time our work has been going on, for the imperfect maps which have been issued. And this state of things will go on indefinitely, unless put a stop to by the State by continuing our work to completion; because it is for the interest of the parties engaged in this business to have an excuse for issuing new maps as often as possible, just as milliners and dealers in dry goods arrange their business so that the fashions may change every three months at least, ostensibly for the benefit of the ladies, but really for their own, and to the great detriment of the unfortunate husbands.

It may be said, also, that the United States surveys will give us, eventually, a correct map of the State, and that it is therefore unnecessary for us to do it: this is not the case, for a most careful examination of the United States work shows clearly that it can never, in a mountainous country like California, be coaxed into anything like a permanently valuable map. The town and section lines are run in the valleys, it is true, and were this State a vast plain, these lines would give us a general idea of the country, as they have in the great Mississippi Valley; but, in a region like our State, of which less than one-fifth of the surface is plain or valley, they are of no account at all, especially as topography is no part of the idea of the Government in having the lines run, while the work itself (most of it, at least) is so carelessly and even fraudulently done that it is impossible to make it fit together. In making accurate surveys of regions where the town and section lines have been run by the Government, we have found sometimes that a line supposed to be a mile in length, and measured as such in the United States linear survey, was in reality a mile and three-quarters long, so that the net-work of Government lines, when laid down on the paper as they actually are, and not as they profess to be, look somewhat as a gridiron struck by lightning might be supposed to. This need not always be the fault of the surveyor, as the system itself is one that is not in the slightest degree applicable to the survey of mountainous countries. In the southern part of this State millions of dollars have been paid for surveys which were in reality never executed, as we find, when we go over the ground, that there is not the least resemblance between the topography as laid down on the official maps and that which our work shows it to be.

Our plan of operations and publication has been carefully adjusted to meet the wants and the means of the State. We propose to publish maps on different scales, all accurate as far as they go, but, of course, with a varying amount of detail, to suit the condition of different sections, basing the amount of detail on the density of the population of the section mapped. For the whole State we take a scale of ten or twelve miles to the inch, which will give us a map about five feet square, and as large a one as can conveniently be used for a wall map for schools and for the people at large. For the central portion of the State we take a scale of six miles to the inch, which gives us four times the area of the other. This central map embraces only one-third the area of the State, but it includes over ninety per cent. of the population. This map is well under way, the field-work being about four-fifths and the drawing one-half done. It can be completed entirely in the next two years, with a reasonable appropriation, and when done will be the largest inland piece of map-work yet undertaken in the country, as it will give the details of the topography of 80,000 square miles of territory—an area nearly twice that of Ohio. The same scale is adopted for the Coast Ranges south of Monterey as far as Los Angeles, and this map is about two-thirds completed.

For the most thickly settled parts of the State we have adopted a much larger scale, of two miles to an inch namely, giving an area of nine times that of the last mentioned map for the same territory. Of the work done on this scale you have before you a sample, which will render it unnecessary for me to go into any details in regard to it, and which will enable every man to judge for himself of the value of the survey maps. The one in question is the Map of the Vicinity of the Bay of San Francisco, of which a large supply is now on the way from New York, in different styles of mounting.

Of the belt of mining counties along the Sierra Nevada, three maps on this scale are in preparation : one, that of Plumas and Sierra, is done as to the field-work, and the drawing of it will be completed during the winter, so that it can be engraved next summer if our work goes on. The central counties, from Nevada to Calaveras, are also well under way, and the southern begun ; the rate of progress will depend, of course, on the amount of funds provided by this Legislature for the continuance of our work.

According to my calculations the whole of the map-work can be completed in four years, if pushed with vigor, and I consider that, taking all things into consideration, it may be considered now as nearly half done. The question, therefore, before you is, not whether a topographical survey of the State shall be made ; but whether, one having been commenced on the authority of one and continued on that of four successive Legislatures until nearly half done, it shall be abandoned just as its results are beginning to be laid before the people.

It is intended that all the maps published by the Survey shall be sold singly, mounted according to the fancy of the purchaser, or in plain sheets, and that they shall all, at the close of the work, be collected and bound into a volume forming one of the series of our Report. I do not hesitate to say that they will form a series of which the State may be proud, and which will be considered by persons ac-. quainted with such matters as fully repaying the entire cost of the survey. With the aid of our maps, each county can, by the help of the County Surveyor, and at a comparatively trifling expense, have a special county map of its own, on which such items may be inserted as are peculiarly desirable for county purposes, and which can be taken from the official records with the sanction of the Supervisors.

The geographical discoveries of the Survey in this State have been of great interest, having brought to light much that was new and curious in regard to the peaks, passes, mountains, and valleys of the Coast Ranges and the Sierra. We have opened a new region to the traveller and the tourist, as large as Switzerland, of which the mountain peaks surpass those of the Alps in elevation, and which in grandeur of scenery is without a parallel on the continent. If this region had ever been explored or visited by any one before us, no record exists of such exploration, nor had ever one word been written or published in regard to it, until the Geological Survey made its existence known. And let not the importance of such discoveries be under-estimated. Few persons who have not turned their thoughts in that direction, with some knowledge of what is going on in other parts of the world, have any proper idea of the real value to the State, in a pecuniary point of view, of its natural scenery. Superficial observers may not recognize the fact that the picturesque is an element in the resources of the State as much, if not in as great a degree, as its agricultural and mineral capacity. The time will come when the money brought into this State by pleasure travellers will be, if not as important an element in our prosperity as it is in Switzerland, at least no mean addition to our resources. By opening up our grand scenery, describing and mapping our most picturesque regions, and spreading a knowledge of them through the world, the survey has done the State a great pecuniary service, which will be recognized in the future if it is not now.

The results obtained in the department of Physical Geography, such as the elevations of towns, mining camps, valleys, mountains and passes, the distribution and character of animal life, forest and plant vegetation, climatological data, circumstances bearing on agricultural capacity, and many other points of this kind, are all of great value, not only scientifically, but practically. The records preserved in the office of the survey are constantly being consulted by those who are seeking information in regard to all kinds of public improvements on this coast; and if one-half those who have thus been benefited by our work could appear before you and give their testimony, I have little doubt but that it would furnish an overwhelming mass of evidence in our favor.

In the geological department of the survey, with its subdivisions of general geology, economical geology, and palæontology, good progress has been made, and the way prepared to make a much more rapid advancement in the future, if we have the necessary pecuniary assistance. It seems almost an absurdity, at this late day, to be arguing in favor of a geological examination of a great and little known mining country like that of California. The fact that such surveys have been made in all civilized foreign countries, and in nearly every one of the United States, in many of which this kind of investigations had not one-tenth part of the interest which they have here, is sufficient *prima facie* evidence in favor of their value. The fact, also, that five successive Legislatures have, after due investigation, given their verdict on the importance of this survey, seems to me to offer a very fair guarantee that it was undertaken with sufficient reason, and the only question which ought legitimately to come up, at the present time, would be: Is the work being carried on in a satisfactory manner?

As, however, each Legislature has the power of upsetting that which has been done or begun by its predecessors; and as, therefore, the original question of the propriety of such a work as ours must be started anew and discussed at each session, regardless of all previous indorsements, public or private, I will take the liberty of stating once more what the special aim of the geological part of the survey is, before undertaking to give an account of the progress made in that department of our work.

The strictly geological portions of the survey may be divided into two sections. The first includes the general geology and palæontology; the second, the economical, or applied, geology. Under the first division we include all that relates to the general geological structure of the State, while the second embraces the practical application of the information thus obtained to the wants and uses of the people in the arts, manufactures and commerce. Under the head of general geology, we have to investigate the nature of the different rock formations which are spread out in the valleys or piled up in the immense mountain masses which traverse the State. We endeavor to ascertain of what materials they are composed ; how originally formed or deposited ; what changes they have undergone since their deposition, and by what agencies these changes have been brought about. We search for and describe the fossil remains which the stratified rocks contain, and thus are enabled to compare them with the formations of other countries and to fix their relation, geological age and position. We then trace over the surface of the State and lay down upon the map the range and extent or the geological distribution of the different systems and groups of rocks, and exhibit their stratigraphical relations, or position with regard to each other, by means of sections, showing the configuration of the surface and the character of the rocks beneath it, along certain lines measured and examined for the purpose. By these preliminary operations we are prepared with the necessary basis on which to proceed with the next great division of our work, namely, the economical geology. Without this scientific part of the survey, the practical would have no permanent value, for it would be nothing but an incoherent mass of material such as our newspapers are filled with, not put into form or reduced to system, so as to be generally applicable and easily comprehended. After and while tracing out the various geological formations and getting their sequence thoroughly established, we endeavor to discover and classify the metallic and mineral treasures which they contain, to ascertain their position and mode of occurrence, or, in other words, to gather all the facts necessary to enable us to determine their present and prospective value, and to show how and under what conditions they may be best made available for the industrial purposes of life. In doing this we furnish a basis for detailed explorations for further deposits of metallic and mineral treasures, by limiting the field for research for numerous prospectors always engaged in the search for useful ores, so that every man will be working where his labor will tell, and not throwing it away in undertakings which a comprehensive view of the mode of occurrence and geological position of our economically valuable materials will show to be a mere waste of money, time and energy. I do not hesitate to say that millions have been wasted in this State, for want of just that information which we shall be prepared to supply, and which, indeed, we have already supplied to a considerable extent to those asking for it. Every year sees an addition to the number of persons availing themselves of information, which we are always ready to give, on matters connected with the geological mode of occurrence and the probable value of deposits of all kinds of metal and mineral ; and I know that, in some cases, our advice has been followed with manifest advantage, and that, as time goes on and demonstrates the reliability of our work, and the substantiality of the basis on which our opinions are founded, the survey will be more and more efficient as a break on the wheel of reckless mining expenditures. If this survey could have been begun at an early period in the development of the State, and have firmly established itself in the confidence of the people at the time of the last great mining excitement on this coast, of what incalculable value might it not have been! I am aware that there are persons so little acquainted with the principles of political economy and the laws which govern the progress of nations, as to think that money expended in the State is a benefit to it, whether any results of permanent value be attained or not by such expenditure. Benjamin Franklin had a clearer idea of the truth when he put into the mouth of Poor Richard his famous saying : "A penny saved is a penny earned." It is only in communities where the pence are saved that the great results of a permanent and high civilization are obtained. To insure permanent working and economical development of what is discovered, by giving every one the means of knowing beforehand how his discoveries may be turned to the best account, how he can best open his mine, how treat his ores, what form to give his products and where and in what quantity they can be disposed of — these are some of the more important points to be gained by the development of that department of our work which is included under the designation of Economical Geology. The services which we shall be able to render, in this line, will become every day more important, as our basis of experience is enlarged and as it becomes more clearly understood that our opinions are disinterested, and that we have no other objects in view than the welfare of the State and the development of its mineral resources. In our volumes devoted to Economical Geology we shall throw all possible light on these subjects, and it will not be our fault if the man about to embark in any undertaking connected with ores or mineral substances shall not find in our book something which shall materially aid him in his undertaking, or at least prevent a foolish waste of money on the impracticable. It is, in every respect, desirable also that the resources of the State should be made known to the world, under official guarantee of correctness, so that not only our own capitalists, but those of other countries, should have opened to them a field for investment, in regard to which they may under. stand that they have some substantial basis of facts and reliable data for generalization, and not feel that they are entering blindfolded into a hap-hazard game of speculation, as is too often the case when putting their money into mines in regions known only from the descriptions of those personally and pecuniarily interested.

In the geological department proper of the survey, one volume has already been published, which, under the title of "A Report of Progress and Synopsis of the Field-work from 1861 to 1864, inclusive," gives the results of a general reconnaissance of the State, both geological and geographical. In this volume the main features of our physical geography and geology will be found delineated, exclusively from the results of our own observations, and with them is incorporated a considerable amount of general information with regard to our mineral resources, incidentally brought in, as also notices of our natural scenery, botany, distribution of forests, etc., all of which subjects will eventually be more elaborately treated in special volumes ; so that this might be considered rather in the light of a temporary report than as a part of a final series. To close the general geology another volume will be required, and is in process of preparation. This will give a systematic and thorough review of the geological structure of the State, and will be fully illustrated by geological maps and sections, which were necessarily wanting in the first volume, and which will be a text-book for the student in this department, and a reliable guide to those who, from whatever motive, shall desire to make themselves acquainted with the course of events which has given its present configuration and internal structure to that part of the continent which we inhabit.

In Palæontology, we have published one volume, and another is well on the way, a considerable part of the plates being already engraved and the text stereotyped. A third volume will be necessary to enable us to describe the remarkable animals which lived on this coast just before the present epoch, including the elephant, mastodon, camel, tapir, horse (of several species now extinct), buffalo, rhinoceros, hippopotamus, and others of remarkable and little-known genera ; also, the forest vegetation of that epoch, of which the remains now lie buried in our deep gravel deposits, and which differed entirely from that which we now see occupying the flanks of the Sierra ; also, the microscopic organisms of which a large portion of our rocks are almost entirely made up, and which can be shown to have a very important bearing in an economical point of view, as constituting the origin and source of the bituminous matter, asphaltum and petroleum, so widely distributed over the State.

In the department of Economical Geology, less progress has been made than would be desirable, partly on account of the necessity of its being preceded by the other departments, in order that it may have a safe basis on which to stand ; but more because the appropriations have been insufficient. It stands to reason that the necessary assistance to thoroughly work up this department cannot be had without paying for it. Men qualified to do this work can obtain large salaries as heads of mines and mills ; and, if asked to give their services to the State for half or quarter of what they can obtain elsewhere, are very apt to see it in another light than that of exclusive devotion to science regardless of personal considerations. And if I should take young men and educate them until they became competent for the work, I very much fear that the result would recall to mind the modern reading of an old text : "Train up a child and away he goes."

The first volume in this department is, however, well under way and can soon be put to press ; it will contain the non-metalliferous minerals occurring in the State, that is to say, all materials used as fuel, for illuminating, or for building purposes, including coal, asphaltum, petroleum, lime, cement, plaster, marble, granite, and the whole long list of substances of mineral origin used in the arts, and not in the metallic form. A most careful examination has been made of all localities where bituminous materials of any kind occur in considerable quantity ; specimens have been collected and subjected to chemical analysis ; new processes have been contrived for making them available, and the results, when fully reported, cannot fail to interest all who are turning their attention in the direction of available fuel and illuminating materials. The coal interests of this coast are also of great importance ; they require and have received a large share of attention.

We come next to the Natural History department of the survey. This is divided into botany and zoölogy, as before stated, having for its object a complete description of all the forms of animal and vegetable life occurring naturally within our borders.

The department of Botany was under the direction of Professor Brewer, now of Yale College, while he was in this State, and is now, so far as the working up of the flowering plants and publication of the results obtained is concerned. Ever since the commencement of the Survey, a vigorous collection of materials has been going on, first under the direction of Professor Brewer, and now of Mr. Bolander. This collecting, carried on in all quarters of the State, has furnished a vast mass of materials, including a great number of entirely new genera and species, and these have been distributed to the most eminent botanists in the country to be worked up—an operation which has been going on steadily for the last three or four years—the work being so far advanced towards completion that it is thought that the volume of flowering plants may be put to press towards the close of the present year ; but that, at all events, it can be finished and printed in time for delivery to the next Legislature.

In Zoölogy there are four volumes under way, and in different stages of preparation, the text of all being well advanced, and nothing required to enable them to be put to press excepting the completion of the illustrations, the drawing and engraving of which has been going on for more than three years.

Having now given a rapid sketch of the general progress of our work, and shown something of the results accomplished in each department, and of what more is proposed to be done, provided we are furnished with the means, I will proceed to discuss a few points connected with the existence and completion of the Survey, a little more in detail than I have been able to do in the preceding systematic review.

Assuming that the plan of the Survey is a good one, and judiciously contrived, the question arises—how is it being carried out? Forming a plan is one thing, and executing it another. To this question I can only reply that our work, as far as accomplished, has been submitted to those who would unanimously, among scientific men, be regarded as best qualified to judge of such matters, and has met with their warm and decided approval. I have assumed that if the survey was done in such a manner as to win the applause of the highest authority in science, in this country, that I might consider it as being well done. And when I say highest authorities, I mean such men as Professor Bache, the late eminent Superintendent of the Coast Survey, Dana of Yale College, Agassiz and Gray, of Harvard, Henry and Baird of the Smithsonian, Lea and Leidy of Philadelphia, Guyot of Princeton, etc. From all of these, letters are on file at our office, expressing sentiments of the warmest interest and the most entire satisfaction in regard to our work, and which are at the service of any member of the Legislature to read and examine. I will take the liberty of reading part of one myself. It is from one of the heads of the Smithsonian Institution, and addressed to the State Geologist, under date of October 18, 1865 :

"Volume I of the Geological Report of California is a work of which the State may well be proud, as, while of almost unrivaled typographical execution, its contents are of the first order of scientific merit. It needs but the full completion of your plans in regard to the entire series to give to the Pacific slope of the United States an encyclopædia of information respecting its natural and physical history far more perfect and complete than is possessed by any other State in the Union, New York even not excepted. You may safely assure the Governor and Legislature of California—if such indorsement is necessary—that there are no dissentient views among the men of science here as regards their interest in the Survey in its various branches, and their satisfaction with the character of its plans and execution, as far as it has gone."

To this it might, however, be answered by the opponents of the Survey that a jury of scientific men is not the proper kind of a one to sit in judgment on this work. If that be the case, then I am not the proper kind of a person to carry on the Survey; and to adopt such a principle, or suggest any other tribunal than a scientific one, would be at once to destroy all that gives character and respectability to our work. We assume that those men who have devoted their whole lives to investigations of this kind, and attained the highest positions and universal recognition as representative men in science, are best qualified to judge in regard to the value of work done in their respective departments, and that if the authority of their opinions is not appreciated by the people at large, it is because the people have not arrived at a sufficiently high stage of educational development to understand what is for their own interests. But I do not mean to be understood as saying that non-professional men have not given us their hearty support in many cases, and that the Survey is only appreciated by the few. On the contrary, we have received the most satisfactory assurances of sympathy and regard for our work, and of its practical value, from many who would not claim to be considered as other than practical men themselves. The only difficulty, as before hinted, has been to induce the opponents of the Survey to give our work a candid examination, or any examination at all. They have conceived a blind prejudice, based on some little matters which have no relation to the real merits or plan of the survey, and have acted accordingly, entirely regardless of the fact that, if successful in their opposition, they would be incurring an amount of odium which every year's advance of the State toward a higher plane of civilization would not fail to increase.

The question of the establishment of a State University is again before the Legislature of California, and this time in a more tangible form than ever before. Indeed it is understood that a site has been selected, and there seems to be a general calling from all quarters for some positive action which shall set the wheels in motion. In view of these facts, I deem it more than ever justifiable in me to call attention to the fact that the Geological Survey is a necessary preliminary to the establishment of a University which can claim to be anything more than a name.

It is not from the standpoint of a Professor, or from any supposed right to be heard, based on an intimate acquaintance with the organization and management of several of our higher institutions of learning, including both those connected with the various State Governments, and those independent of them—those counting the years of their existence by hundreds, and the amount of their endowment by millions, and those whose career has but just begun, and who are proportionately short of funds—it is not, I say, on any such grounds as these that I approach the subject ; but simply as one called before you to defend the Geological Survey, and who desires, as one of the important points in this defense, to urge upon you the educational relations of our proposed work, not only as connected with the proposed University, but with all our schools and institutions of learning. For I take it that there is no institution of so low a grade that the leading facts of the geography of the State should not be taught in it, and that we should not have to rise very high in order to come to those in which instruction should be given in the elements, at least, of natural history. But it is to the proposed University that I especially refer, as our work is more intimately connected with that than with institutions of a lower grade.

In a University established under the conditions which surround us on the Pacific coast, it is not difficult to see that the practical will have very much the upper hand over the theoretical and abstruse ; that modern languages will outweigh the ancient, and that the natural and physical sciences will be more cultivated than psychology and metaphysics. There will be little call for Latin and less for Greek ; but nature will be interrogated, and everything that aids in familiarizing the student with her teachings will be in demand. The scientific branches in which instruction will be most craved by the student, will certainly be physical geography, geology, mineralogy, botany and zoölogy; these at least will be departments which as much if not more than any other it will be necessary to have filled, if the proposed institution is to have any rank at all, or to be in any respect up to the standard of other colleges, universities or schools of science. Make the institution as practical as you please, lower its grade to the last conceivable degree, still the great fact cannot be got over that something has to be taught there; that there must be some course of study, and that whether you simplify or complicate the programme, the already mentioned branches will be the last to be omitted from it.

Now I state what I know to be a fact, when I assert that no one of the branches in question can be taught in any other than the most superficial way until the results of our Survey are in the hands of the teachers. This statement I will illustrate by reference to our botanical work, as this may probably be better understood by the people generally than any of the other departments mentioned. It will probably be admitted by all that it would be absolutely necessary for the teacher of botany, in order to impart to the student anything more than the merest rudiments of the science, to know the names and position in the system of the plants which grow in his vicinity, and which he would collect and use for illustration of his teachings, and which his pupils would bring to him for that purpose. This knowledge, however, is an impossibility at present; there is no botanist in the State who can name the plants he collects, nor is there any one person elsewhere who can do it for him.

The facts are simply these: During the last seventy years, more than one hundred and twenty professional botanists and collectors have visited parts of the regions west of the Rocky Mountains, and more than seventy of them have traveled in California. Their collections have gone into the various herbaria of this country and of Europe, and the printed data relating to them are scattered through an immense number of volumes; so that if any one were to begin and make a complete collection of them, it would require years of labor and thousands of dollars expenditure, and, even with the most strenuous exertions, it would be impossible to make the list complete. But if this could be done, and this library could be transferred to the Pacific coast and placed in their possession, our botanists would still be unable to give correct names to their specimens. And for these reasons: not unfrequently several collectors have obtained the same species in different localities and seasons and in varying forms; specimens thus collected have been referred to different botanists for description, the amount of material being often meager and insufficient, and the results have been published at places widely remote from each other. Thus, what was in reality one and the same species, has often several names attached to it ; but to discover this fact and clear up all the difficulties, so that all the synonyms should be properly arranged under the real name, or the one having priority, according to the universally recognized rules of scientific nomenclature, requires not only the extensive collections of the Survey, made under the most favorable circumstances, in all kinds of localities, and under all conditions of growth, but also an actual inspection and diligent study of the original specimens collected by all botanists prior to our work. These are, luckily, mostly accessible in the grand herbarium at Cambridge, which Professor Gray, the leading botanist of the country, has for the past forty years been gathering together. Without the aid of this gentleman it would be impossible for any one to get through with the immense undertaking of bringing order into the chaos of California botany. And not only has he kindly lent us the use of his herbarium and library, and given his personal attention to the description of the great number of new plants collected by our parties, but the same may be said of every other eminent botanist in this country: Engelmann, Torrey, Eaton, Tuckerman, Lesquereux and Thurber, as well as several of the most distinguished authorities in Europe, have lent us a hand in unraveling the twisted skein, and one gentleman is about to leave his home in a western city and visit Europe for the purpose of comparing specimens of the California pines and oaks with the authentically named ones existing in the herbaria in England and on the Continent. I should add, lest anybody's sensibilities be alarmed by the excessive expenditure, that he receives no salary, and travels at his own expense.

We shall thus have a work, in the botanical department, in which each plant, in every important group of families, will be authentically named by the highest authority in that section of the science—a book which every student can use with perfect confidence in its reliability, and which will be the indispensable guide of every teacher of the science. And we could not have had it in any other way than this : it required a combined effort of all the botanists in the country, sanctioned by the State, to do this work ; and with all the facilities the survey affords, this task is an arduous one.

The same thing may be said (*mutatis mutandis*) with regard to the other scientific branches mentioned. I will not tire you by going through them all, but will merely add that great pains have been taken with the illustrations of the natural history volumes to make them such as will, while possessing a high scientific value, be most useful to students. And at the same time economy has been studied, so that I am fully justified in assuring you that, while our series will be more complete than those of any other State, they will also have cost much less.

In fact, this idea has been constantly in my mind, while engaged in the Survey, that our work was the necessary preliminary of the University and the cultivation of science on this coast in general, and I have endeavored so to shape our plans that when our task has been completed the way shall be smoothed for others to carry on that which we have begun ; for so inexhaustible on this is nature in her ways and works, that we cannot look forward to any time when the student can fold his hands for want of something to do, in the way of enlarging the boundaries of either natural or physical science.

I need not enlarge on the importance of our full and authentically named collections, in the various departments, to the State University. They will form the foundation of a museum invaluable for the purposes of instruction, and such a one as could not have been brought together without a thorough and systematic plan of operations. The collections are amply sufficient to justify their being divided, and I trust that when they pass out of our hands they may be made as available as possible, both for scientific and popular instruction. This can be best accomplished by giving one series to the University, and the other to the Academy of Sciences, in San Francisco, in which latter place a museum will be accessible to a much larger number of persons than it would be anywhere else, and where our materials would be added to a large and rapidly increasing collection, in charge of the only scientific association on the coast, and which, in time and with the growth of a liberal and scientific spirit in this State, will have the means to display them in a suitable manner and to preserve them from destruction.

Finally, I conceive that the Survey ought to be carried on because it has been begun—not only because it has been indorsed by several successive Legislatures, and by eminent scientific authority at home and abroad, but that the State may not be making an exhibition of herself, in the eyes of the world, as a specimen of fickleness and unreliability. Having published far and wide that we were going to have a thorough geological survey, and having been liberally patted on the back for our energy and far-sightedness, I can conceive of nothing more humiliating than backing down, without reason, when the work is already more than half completed, and the most practically valuable portion of the results is just beginning to see the light. I am aware that there are some who would pull the survey up by the roots in order that the University may be planted in the same hole, with the idea that there would be economy in that operation, or else with some hidden notion that does not appear on the surface. There might have been some reason in this plan of making the Survey by the University, or a University out of the Survey, for the two things amount to about the same, had it been put in operation at the commencement of our work. Indeed, something like this was suggested by the State Geologist, three years ago, in an official report. It is now too late : as organized, the Survey requires the entire thoughts and time of every man connected with it, and there has never been a new College or University established in the country where the Professors had not their hands full in attending to their legitimate official duties, and few is the number of them who are fitted by education or practice to engage in a work such as we are carrying on, without special preliminary training. To stop the Survey in order to encourage the University would be like pulling the foundation of a building to pieces in order to get material for the walls and roof.

By what I have said here to-night, I am aware that I have laid myself open to the charge of blowing my own trumpet ; but in what I have said I am very sure that I have not exceeded the truth, and that I have not given an opinion not backed by many years of experience. I cannot refrain from adding, however, that I have carried on this Survey in spite of many obstacles and great temptations to engage in other less laborious and responsible, but more lucrative, work. Enough has been accomplished to show to the world what it would be were my plans to be carried out, and thus to take from my shoulders the responsibility of the failure if the Legislature chooses to bring the work to an end. If the Survey can be continued on the same basis on which it has thus far been prosecuted, free from all political contaminations, and with the same ideal of thoroughness, and with a sufficient liberal appropriation to insure a rapid carrying on of the work, I shall rejoice to go on with it and complete it, as I fully believe that it will reflect the highest credit on the State, and all officially connected with it, as well as the Legislatures by which it has been upheld. Let the work stop, without any fault or *laches* of mine, and I shall feel that it is not of me that it can be said that, "having put his hand to the plow, he looked back."

Letter of the State Geologist

RELATIVE TO THE PROGRESS OF THE

STATE GEOLOGICAL SURVEY,

DURING

THE YEARS 1864-65.

LETTER.

SAN FRANCISCO, January 1, 1866.

To His Excellency, F. F. Low,
    Governor of California:

SIR :—The Legislature, during the session of eighteen hundred and sixty-three and eighteen hundred and sixty-four, re-established the office of State Geologist, then about to expire by constitutional limitation, by passing the following Act:

"AN ACT

TO CREATE THE OFFICE OF STATE GEOLOGIST, AND TO DEFINE THE DUTIES THEREOF.

" *The People of the State of California, represented in Senate and Assembly, do enact as follows:*

"SECTION 1. J. D. Whitney is hereby appointed State Geologist. He shall be commissioned by the Governor, and it shall be his duty, with the aid of such assistants as he may appoint, to complete the geological survey of the State, and prepare a report of said survey for publication, and superintend the publication of the same. Such report shall be in the form of a geological, botanical, and zoological history of the State; and the number of copies of each volume to be printed, and the style, form, maps, diagrams, or illustrations to be contained therein, or to be printed separately, shall be determined by the State Geologist; and said report, when published, shall be sold upon such terms as the Governor and Secretary of State may decide upon, and the proceeds of such sales shall be paid into the Common School Fund of the State.

"SEC. 2. It is hereby made the duty of the State Geologist and his assistants to devote the time not necessarily required in the preparation and superintendence for publication of the reports provided for in section one of this Act, to a thorough and scientific examination of the gold, silver, and copper producing districts of this State, and to such scientific and practical experiments as will be of value in the discovery of mines and the working and reduction of ores.

"Sec. 3. The following sums of money are hereby appropriated, out
of any money in the State Treasury not otherwise appropriated, for
the prosecution of the geological survey of the State, and for the sixteenth and seventeenth fiscal years : For salary of the State Geologist,
nine thousand dollars, to be drawn monthly on the last day of each month;
for salary of two assistants, six thousand six hundred dollars, to be drawn
in the same manner as the salary of the State Geologist; for publication
of two volumes of report, six thousand dollars; for office rent, and
expenses of survey in mining districts, and experiments on ores, and all
incidental expenses of work, ten thousand dollars, to be drawn one half
each fiscal year.
"Sec. 4. This Act shall take effect immediately."

The above Act was approved by the Governor, April fourth, eighteen
hundred and sixty-four.
Previous to the passage of this Act the following sums had been
appropriated for the continuance of the survey :

At the time of the passage of the original Act............	$20,000
By the Legislature of 1860–61...........................:	15,000
By the Legislature of 1861–62...............................	15,000
By the Legislature of 1862–63...............................	20,000
Making in all...................................	$70,000

Besides this, three thousand dollars was appropriated by the Legislature of eighteen hundred and sixty-one and sixty-two for printing one
volume of the report.
At the time the Legislature of eighteen hundred and sixty-three and
sixty-four met the new Constitution of the State was in operation, and
the sessions being now biennial, instead of annual, it was necessary to
provide funds for continuing the survey for two years. Unfortunately
the State was at this time in great trouble, the drought of the two previous winters having most seriously affected both the agricultural and
mining interests, and given rise to a widespread feeling of alarm. It
was therefore with difficulty that any appropriation could be secured for
the survey, and that which was obtained was far from being adequate to
the carrying on of the work on a scale commensurate with its importance. Indeed, it was but just enough to keep the survey alive, in
addition to continuing the preparation of the materials already in hand
for publication. The appropriations for the survey in the Act cited
above, added to those of previous Legislatures, make the total amount
provided for the field work and salaries in all departments, from the commencement of the survey up to June thirtieth, eighteen hundred and sixty-
six, ninety-five thousand six hundred dollars, or a little less than sixteen
thousand dollars a year on the average. Besides this, however, there
has been nine thousand dollars appropriated for publication, which should
not be charged to the survey, as this amount will be refunded to the
State by the sale of the volumes published, it being provided in both
Acts that our publications shall be sold and the money paid into the
Common School Fund.
The course and progress of the geological and topographical fieldwork

of the survey, up to the end of the year eighteen hundred and sixty-three, has already been made known in the letters addressed to the Governor from year to year. A resumé of the movements of the various parties will also be found in the preface of the first volume of the geology of the report.

In the summer of eighteen hundred and sixty-four, a small party was fitted out to commence the exploration of the Sierra Nevada, it being my intention to work up the geology and topography of that great chain, from the south towards the north, as accurately as our time and means would allow. This party consisted of Messrs. Brewer and Hoffman, accompanied by Messrs. King and Gardner, volunteer assistants in the geological and topographical departments. They took the field in May, and proceeded across the plains of the San Joaquin to Visalia, from which point they entered the Sierra, ascending King's River to its source, and exploring the whole region about the headwaters of that and Kern River. Thence they made their way across the range by a pass over twelve thousand feet high, passed up Owen's Valley, ascended the west branch of Owen's River, crossing the Sierra again at an altitude of twelve thousand four hundred feet, and thence descending to the head of the San Joaquin River. The exploration was continued through the region of the headwaters of that stream and the Merced, connecting the reconnoisance with that of eighteen hundred and sixty-three around the sources of the Tuolumne. The whole expedition occupied about three months, during which time the geography and geology of a district including an area of over ten thousand square miles were for the first time explored, the whole region having previously been entirely unknown. The results prove to be of the greatest interest, disclosing the fact that this was the highest part of the Sierra Nevada, and that it embraced the loftiest mountains and the grandest scenery yet discovered within the territory of the United States. For the details of this reconnoisance reference may be made to Chapter X of Volume I of the Geology, which has just been published by the survey.

At the close of this campaign Professor Brewer relinquished his position on the survey, and left California to enter on his duties as Professor in the Sheffield Scientific School of Yale College. He still remains, however, charged with the direction of the botanical department of the survey, as will be noticed further on, under the head of botany.

Messrs. King and Gardner continued their explorations northward of the field of their labor during the summer, by making a survey and map of the Yosemite Valley, under authority of the Commissioners appointed to take charge of the tracts embracing that valley and the Big Tree Grove of Mariposa County, recently conveyed to the State of California by the United States.

In the spring of eighteen hundred and sixty-four, Mr. King had commenced the detailed exploration of the principal metalliferous belt of the Sierra Nevada, by examining the geology of the Mariposa estate and its vicinity. This work was continued by Mr. Rémond in the summer of eighteen hundred and sixty-five, and carried from the Merced to the Stanislaus River, a careful geological and geographical map of that region having been furnished by him as the result of his labors. In addition to this he visited and examined seventy-seven gold mines, besides many other localities of other metals, and sixty-six quartz mills, of which twenty-three were in operation. This work, which is the continuation of that done in the Sierra during the previous year, forms the first contribution to our detailed exploration of the mining districts of

California; this exploration we expect to continue as soon as it is in our power to take the field again in the Sierra.

In the meantime, Mr. Gabb has left for the southern part of the State, to make a thorough examination of portions of the Coast Ranges, where the occurrence of bituminous matter in large quantity has, especially during the last twelve months, been exciting much attention.

The above is all the geological fieldwork which it has been in our power to undertake, with the extremely limited appropriation made by the last Legislature, a portion of which had necessarily to be used in the preparation of the "Geological, Botanical, and Zoological History of the State," provided for in the Act under which we are now at work. What progress has been made in the preparation of our results for publication, in conformity with the Act, will now be stated under the appropriate heads.

I.—TOPOGRAPHY.

In addition to the maps previously described as forming a portion of the results of our topographical work, we have commenced a new one, which embraces the most valuable and important part of the State, and covers the area on which, as near as can be ascertained, somewhat over nine tenths of the population are now residing. This map extends from the parallel of thirty-six degrees and thirty minutes to that of forty degrees and thirty minutes, and from the one hundred and eighteenth to the one hundred and twenty-third meridian, thus including the whole Sierra from Owen's Lake north, to Lassen's Peak, the Coast Ranges from Point Sur and New Idria on the south, to Clear Lake on the north. It also includes the western portion of Nevada. The scale of this map is six miles to the inch, and its size four and a half feet square, so that it can be engraved to four sheets. On this all the topographical work of the survey has been compiled, together with such materials of an authentic character as could be obtained from other sources, especially from the offices of the United States Surveyor-General, and the United States Coast Survey. The work of Mr. Wackenreuder in the high Sierra, which was continued for a short time during the summer of eighteen hundred and sixty-four, forms an important portion of the new material incorporated in our map of Central California. The drawing of this map is considerably advanced, and has been executed by Mr. Hoffman, the topographer of the survey, in the most creditable manner; if ever completed, it will not only form a highly important contribution to the geography of the State, but will be of great practical value. A considerable amount of fieldwork, however, remains to be done in the region which it covers. The extreme northwestern portion, including the region north of Clear Lake, has never been even approximately mapped, and portions of the Sierra, especially the region between the Mono and the Silver Mountain Passes, and that north of the Henness Pass, have never been instrumentally surveyed.

The "map of the region adjacent to the Bay of San Francisco," and that of the vicinity of Mont Diablo, are ready to be placed in the engraver's hands, and the last named one will be photolithographed as soon as an establishment for doing this kind of work by the "Osborne process" is set in operation in this country, Mr. Osborne being at present in Boston for this purpose. Some difficulty has been met with in finding an artist who could be trusted to do justice to the bay map; but the close of the war and the contraction of the currency will, it is to be presumed, relieve our engravers on copper and steel from a large portion of the calls which have for the last four years been made upon them, and it is probable that this map will be put in hand immediately.

The preparation of a map of the whole State, on a scale of six miles to the inch, was formerly contemplated; but of later years we have considered that this was an undertaking of too extensive a character to meet with encouragement from the Legislature. Should the survey be continued for three or four years longer, we should be able to furnish a general map of California on a scale of ten or twelve miles to the inch, which would far surpass in value and accuracy anything now existing. Still, many years must elapse before correct maps of the almost unknown southeastern and northwestern corners of the State will be had. It is certain that the United States Land Office surveys of the southern part of the State do not give any idea of its topography, and it is difficult to understand how the town and section lines can have been run there, and so little idea of the topography obtained; while the extremely rough and mountainous character of Del Norte, Humboldt, and Trinity Counties, now to a large extent in possession of hostile and warlike Indians, will render it difficult to execute any detailed geological or geographical work in that region, for a long time to come.

II.—PHYSICAL GEOGRAPHY.

Our materials in this department are constantly accumulating; but we have not yet began to arrange them for publication. The barometrical measurements of mountains have been continued, and instruments have been carried to greater heights than ever before were attained within the limits of the United States. We await with much interest the elaborate report of Colonel R. S. Williamson, of the United States Engineers, to the Topographical Bureau, on the subject of the laws governing the fluctuations of the barometer on the Pacific coast. This work will be of great importance to science, and of especial value to us, as enabling us to use our own observations more intelligently than would be possible unless we had the means of carrying on a series of investigations similar to those of Colonel Williamson, and on which a large amount of time and labor would have to be expended. The subject of the distribution of the forest vegetation of the State will occupy a chapter in our volume of Physical Geography, and it is hoped that we shall be able to illustrate it with a map showing the range of the different groups of species.

III.—GENERAL GEOLOGY AND PALÆONTOLOGY.

The volume just issued, which is entitled "Geology—Volume I; a report of progress and synopsis of the fieldwork from 1860 to 1864," will be a sufficient exhibit of our progress in the investigation of the geological structure of the State.

It is to this department of general geology that up to the present time by far the greater portion of our attention has been given, since the first thing required in a geological survey is a knowledge of the general geological structure of the State, the age of the various formations which occur in it, and their range and extent, or the position which they occupy on the surface, and their relations to each other. Each group of strata, thus determined by its lithological peculiarities, and by the fossils which it contains, is then to be laid down upon the map in the position which its outcrop occupies on the surface. The general character of the minerals and ores which occur in each formation or group of strata having been first determined, the details of their mode of occurrence, their relative abundance, and the facilities which may exist in each separate district for making them economically available, must, after the preliminary general work has been done, be the object of more special and detailed examinations. It is not, however, the business of a geological surveying corps to act to any considerable extent as a prospecting party; to do this would require that we should confine our operations to a very limited area. The labor of the whole corps for an entire season would not suffice to throughly prospect more than a few hundred square miles in a very rich mineral region, and we should often have to engage in expensive mining operations to decide what was really of permanent value. It is our task, rather, to limit the field of research, and to show to others where their labor will be best bestowed, preventing foolish expenditure of time and money in searching for what our general geological investigations have determired not to exist in sufficient quantity in certain formations to be worth working. Especially in the first years of our work in a State of such immense area as California, our labors must have more the character of a geological reconnoissance than of a detailed survey.

In the department of palæontology one volume has already been published. This contains, in the first section, a description of the carboniferous fossils of Bass' Ranch, the only locality where any well preserved organic remains of that age have been found within the State. The second section is devoted to the fossils of the triassic rocks, including all which have thus far been discovered in California and on its borders. While we have abundant evidence that a formation equivalent in geological age to the Alpine trias, or the beds of Hallstadt and St. Cassian, occurs over a vast area, and forms an important part of the metalliferous belt of the Pacific coast, and probably on both sides of the Sierra, and while fossils of this age have been found at several localities within the borders of California, our most ample supply of well preserved specimens has come from the Humboldt mining district in Nevada. Hence we have included in our descriptions of the triassic fossils those of that region, although some among them have not yet been found in California.

The third section of the volume of palæontology is devoted to the jurassic fossils of the Sierra Nevada, or, rather, to such as had been discovered at the time of its publication. These fossils are all from the localities near Genessee Valley, noticed in section eleven, Chapter IX of Volume I, of the Geology. At the end of that volume a few pages will be found containing descriptions of the jurassic fossils of the auriferous slates in Mariposa County, from the localities discovered by Mr. King, and in close proximity to one of the great quartz veins of the mining region proper. This paper, by Mr. Meek, and which is illustrated by a steel plate, was published in the geological volume to prevent delay, as the question of the geological age of the auriferous slates is one of great interest, and some time will necessarily elapse before the second volume of the palæontology will be ready for publication. In the meantime, and during the past year, Mr. Rémond has traced the belt of fossiliferous jurassic rocks from the Merced River to the Stanislaus, finding several genera and species different from those previously obtained from this formation. These, together with such other fossils of this age as may hereafter be discovered in the State, will be described and published in the second volume of the palæontology.

The fourth section of the volume in question is devoted to the cretaceous fossils, and forms considerably the larger portion of it, as the rocks of this age occupy a very extensive area on the Pacific coast, and are rich in fossils at many localities. A reference to the section in question will show how large an amount of material, new to science, has been derived from the rocks of the cretaceous series, of the existence of which on this coast previous to the commencement of our work but little was definitely known. The first and third sections of the palæontological volume were prepared by Mr. Meek; the second and fourth by Mr. Gabb. The plates are thirty-two in number, partly engraved on steel, and partly on stone, from drawings furnished by the authors of the text. The volume is printed and bound in a very superior manner, and is sold at three dollars and fifty cents per volume, (in cloth,) as determined by yourself and the Secretary of State, which is about the cost of the mechanical execution of the edition. The text is stereotyped, and one thousand copies have been printed, and bound in various styles. A statement of the number of copies of each volume of the publications of the survey which have been sold, and of the number remaining on hand, will be furnished to the Treasurer of State at the close of each fiscal year; and, at the same time, the money received from the sales will be paid over to that officer, unless otherwise directed by the Legislature, to be placed by him in the Common School Fund of the State. The stereotype plates of the volume remain for the present in charge of the printer.

The first part of Section 1, Volume II, of the Palæontology, is in the hands of the printer. It contains the first portion of the descriptions of the tertiary invertebrate fossils, by Mr. Gabb, and will soon be in circulation. The plates to accompany this article, thirteen in number, are drawn, and will soon be put in hand. A considerable amount of new material from rocks of the cretaceous age is also on hand and partly prepared for the printer and engraver. The vertebrate fossils collected by the survey have been referred to Doctor J. Leidy for description. They will be worked up by him for the second volume of the Palæontology, and in the meantime a preliminary notice of them has been received, containing descriptions of several new species of the fossil horse, rhinoceros, and other large animals, and a catalogue of the whole collection, which comprises remains of the mastodon, elephant, tapir, bison, a reptile allied to the ichthyosaurus, crocodile, and other animals of great interest. The fossil plants of the survey will be worked up by Doctor Newberry, to whom portions of our materials in this department have already been referred. The diatoms and other microscopic forms have been submitted to Mr. A. M. Edwards, of New York. The fauna and flora of the tertiary rock, with the additional matter belonging to the lower formations, which has been and will be obtained before the close of our work, will furnish ample material for a second volume in the palæontological department.

IV.—ECONOMICAL GEOLOGY, MINING, AND METALLURGY.

In the geological volume just published, a considerable amount of information will be found in regard to the economical geology of the State; but all the detailed descriptions of mining regions and mining processes have been reserved for the volume or volumes specially devoted to these subjects. We have now arrived at a stage of the survey when, the preliminary reconnoisance of the State being well advanced, we can take up the mining districts, work up the details of their geology, and investigate the quantity, quality, and mode of occurrence of their ores. We need, however, a laboratory, where the necessary chemical work of this and other branches of the survey can be done, under my immediate personal supervision.

Mr. Ashburner's investigations of the quartz mines and mills of the State were the commencement of work in this department, and, as far as they go, they form an important contribution to an understanding of the mining interests of California. The tabular statement, prepared by him to exhibit the principal facts connected with the auriferous quartz mills running in eighteen hundred and sixty-one, will always be valuable for reference. It has been printed in the appendix to the volume of geology, for convenient reference.

The work of investigating in detail the geology of the mining regions of the State has been begun, but will require a long time for its completion, so vast is the field and so important are the interests with which this branch of our work is connected. We can do much for the benefit of the people in this department if properly supported by the Legislature; but hasty and superficial work will be of little use. Too large a portion of the resources of California has already been thrown away in foolish mining enterprises, and although the career of reckless speculation may seem to be checked at present, yet the same scenes of wild excitement will be repeated again and again unless reliable information becomes widely disseminated among the people. It is fully time that a stop should be put to a course which has already materially retarded the progress of the State, and which, if persisted in, will bring utter financial ruin upon us.

V.—BOTANY.

The botanical department of the survey has been and still continues under the charge of Professor Brewer. From his investigations it appears that about one thousand six hundred species of flowering plants, (including the higher orders of the flowerless,) and over one hundred species of mosses, have been found growing naturally within the limits of the State or on its immediate borders. In the orders below the mosses in the scale of organization the data are still too imperfect to allow a probable estimate to be made of the number of species.

The collection made by the survey contain about seventy-four per cent of all the species known to exist in this State, and about five per cent of them are new to science, and eleven per cent new to the State—that is, not before found within its borders.

Professor Brewer is now engaged in preparing a report which will be in fact a "Manual of the Botany of California," containing as full descriptions of all the plants of the State as can be given in one volume. Of this the general plan and arrangement will be similar to those of the "Colonial Floras," issued under the auspices of the British Government. Full reference and synonyms will be given of all the species peculiar to the Pacific States, and which occur in California; and a chapter will be added on the general distribution of the plants of the State and their economical value. This volume will form a suitable text book to be used in the schools of the Pacific coast in connection with "Gray's Lessons in Botany" or some other elementary work of a similar character; and it may be added that this science cannot be taught in California until such a manual as the one proposed has been prepared, since the descriptions of the plants of the State are at present scattered through hundreds of volumes, most of which are quite inaccessible to any except the very few who are furnished with costly and extensive botanical libraries. In preparing this volume, a task in which considerable progress has been made by Professor Brewer, he will have the aid of several of the most eminent botanists of the country. Professor Gray, of Cambridge, has kindly offered to work up the large and difficult family of the *Compositæ*; he has also determined most of the species in the collection, and has given every facility for consulting the collections and library of the "Gray Herbarium," of Harvard University. Professor Torrey, of New York, will describe certain orders of the *Apetalæ*, of which he has made a special study. Dr. Englemann, of St. Louis, will prepare the description of the *Cactaceæ*, and render assistance in several other orders to which he has particularly devoted himself. Professor Thurber, of New York, will describe the grasses, and Professor Eaton, of New Haven, the ferns and higher cryptogamic plants. The carices collected during the first two years of the survey were examined and determined by Dr. Booth, of London, just before his death. The herbaria of Professor Torrey, so rich in Pacific coast specimens, and those of the Academy of Natural Sciences of Philadelphia, and of the Smithsonian Institution, have also been freely opened to Professor Brewer for comparison and consultation. The plants in the State collection will all be carefully named, and it is hoped that the Legislature will not much longer delay having them placed where they will be accessible for comparison to all students of this science on the Pacific coast.

It is believed that the botanical volume may be got ready for the press before the close of the year eighteen hundred and sixty-seven.

VI.—ZOOLOGY.

The extensive acquaintance of Doctor Cooper with the fauna of the Pacific coast, obtained previous to his connection with the Geological Survey, has enabled him to prepare a large amount of material for the press, forming the basis of at least four volumes of our report. The following table shows what had been accomplished in the way of zoological collecting up to April first, eighteen hundred and sixty-four, in six of the classes :

	Mammals...	Birds........	Reptiles......	Batrachians	Fishes	Mollusca.....
Number of species known to exist in California.............	110	353	66	18	183	542
Collected by the survey	34	237	33	10	74	507
New to the fauna of California......................................	13	11	10	1	20	211
Not before described...........	2(?)	4	4	....	13	122
Found east of the Mississippi	23	161	....	1(?)	2(?)	29

In some of the classes a considerably larger exhibit of species obtained for the collection could have been made, had it not been deemed advisable by Doctor Cooper not to collect the more common and easily procured species until a suitable place had been provided for the museum of the survey. The mounting of specimens of birds and mammals is so much more satisfactorily done from freshly prepared skins, that the collecting of such species as can be readily obtained in this vicinity may properly be deferred until they can be set up at once in the place they are destined to occupy. The number of specimens illustrating the zoology of the Pacific coast, now in the collection of the survey, may be estimated at between seven thousand and eight thousand.

Of three of the four volumes of the zoological reports the illustrations have been in hand for several months, and it is hoped that they will be so far advanced towards completion that at least two of them may go to press during the year eighteen hundred and sixty-six.

Two volumes of the zoological series will be devoted to the birds and mammals, and Doctor Cooper's manuscript will be carefully revised by Professor Baird, of the Smithsonian Institution, who also has charge, under my general direction, of the execution of the illustrations. We propose to give a figure of one species in each genus of the birds; those which have never before been described or figured being illustrated by large colored figures on steel or stone, and the others by wood cuts. The different species of each genus will be distinguished from each other by diagrams of the head, claws, wings, and other characteristic parts. The mammals will also be fully illustrated, the object being to furnish, in the zoological series, manuals or text books which shall not only have a permanent scientific value, as containing in a condensed and systematic form all that is known of the fauna of the State of California and its borders, but which shall also be practically useful to those persons who may desire to ascertain the names and habits of the animals they may meet with on land or in the waters of the Pacific coast.

The description of the fishes will form a separate volume, and this will be prepared by Mr. Theodore Gill, who will be able to use, not only the materials and notes furnished by Doctor Cooper, but also the extensive collection of the Smithsonian Institution, accumulated during many years of labor by the various naturalists who have devoted themselves to gathering specimens on the Pacific coast in this department. Each species will be illustrated by a carefully drawn and engraved figure, the work being done under Mr. Gills' immediate supervision.

The shells will also afford the material for another volume, Doctor Cooper's collections being very extensive, and comprising nearly two hundred new species. As the eminent conchologist, Mr. P. P. Carpenter, has been for a long time specially devoted to the study of the shells of the Pacific coast, Doctor Cooper's collections have been placed in his hands for study, and it is expected that he will prepare one of the volumes of our zoological series, in which each species will be illustrated by an accurate figure.

The maps and sections, with perhaps some of the more important illustrations of the scenery of the State, should be placed together in one volume or atlas, and this will form the proper conclusion of our series of publications.

According to our plans for publication, as developed in the preceding pages, it will be seen that we contemplate issuing from eleven to thirteen volumes, which are distributed among the different departments of the survey as follows:

13

Physical Geography.....	1
General Geology.....	2
Palæontology.....	2
Economical Geology, Mining, and Metallurgy.....	1 or 2
Botany	1
Zoology....	3 or 4
Maps, sections, etc.....	1
Total.....	11 to 13

Of these, two are already issued, and eight more are in a forward
state of preparation, the illustrations of three of them being nearly all
drawn, and a portion of them already engraved. The amount of time
required to complete the series of thirteen volumes will, of course,
depend upon the vigor with which the work is pushed, and that, again,
on the amount appropriated by the Legislature. With a sufficiently
liberal appropriation, it is probable that the fieldwork may be finished
before the time expires when the office 'of State Geologist will by constitutional limitation cease to exist—April the fourth, eighteen hundred
and sixty-eight. The completion of the printing and engraving will of
course require a longer time; but it will perhaps be reasonable to estimate that within four years, from the present time the full series of
volumes may be in the hands of the public.

No provision has yet been made by the Legislature for the arrangement and exhibition of the collections made by the survey, as was contemplated in the original Act under which our work was commenced.
These collections are already very extensive, embracing many thousand
specimens of rocks, fossils, minerals, and ores, as well as the extremely
important suites in the zoological and botanical departments. All these
specimens are of great value, as illustrating the natural history, the
geological structure, and the mineral resources of the State. Such of
these as have not been required for use in the preparation of our report,
remain packed in boxes and stored away at the office of the survey.
Unfortunately, we were obliged, for want of room, to store a portion of
our specimens in a (so-called) fireproof warehouse in San Francisco,
and these have already been destroyed by fire, entailing a serious loss
on the survey and the State. In view of this calamity, it will not be
necessary for me to enlarge on the necessity of providing a permanent
fireproof building for our collections, as has already been repeatedly
urged by me in my annual communications to the Legislature. The
only official step thus far taken by the Legislature towards the establishment of a State Museum, is the passage of the following resolution
by the Legislature of eighteen hundred and sixty-two and eighteen hundred and sixty-three.

" *Resolved*, by the Assembly, the Senate concurring, That Professor J.
D. Whitney, State Geologist, John Swett, State Superintendent of
Public Instruction, and J. F. Houghton, Surveyor General, be and they
are hereby constituted a Board of Commissioners, to report to the
Legislature on or before the second Monday of December, one thousand
eight hundred and sixty-three, upon the feasibility of establishing a
State University, embracing an Agricultural College, a 'School of Mines,'

14

and a Museum—including the geological collection of this State; and that said Board report such facts and considerations as they may deem important in connection therewith."

In obedience to this requisition of the Legislature, an elaborate report was submitted by the Board of Commissioners as above constituted at the session of eighteen hundred and sixty-three and eighteen hundred and sixty-four. In this report the whole subject of the organization of a State University was thoroughly discussed, and the requirements of the Constitution in this respect duly set forth. The establishment of a State Polytechnic School, having for its object " the professional training of young men in the exact and natural sciences, and their application to arts, manufacture, mining, and agriculture," was strongly recommended to the Legislature. It was also proposed that the collections of the geological survey should be placed in a suitable fireproof building, in which should be ample accommodations for displaying and showing them, as well as room for a library, laboratory, and an office for the survey, together with lecture rooms, and other conveniences necessary for a scientific school, for which purpose the building was to be used after the completion of the survey. This would have been the first step towards the establishment of a State University, provided for long since by the Constitution, and for which funds have been furnished by the United States.

The interest on the money received from the sales of the land given by Congress has thus far been applied to another purpose; but it is evident that the people, through the Legislature, are bound in honor to see that the trust accepted by the State and incorporated in their own Constitution should be sacredly complied with.

In concluding this communication, it may be mentioned that the Act under which the survey is at present conducted does not require the State Geologist to present to the Legislature, through the Governor, or in any other way, any annual report or estimate for the continuance of the survey, as was demanded by the Act under which the survey was originally organized. The State Geologist will, however, be happy to appear before the " Committees on Mines and Mining Interests " of the Senate and House, and to give them all possible information in regard to the progress of the survey, and what he deems desirable for continuing the work both in the field and in the office.

I am, with high respect, your obedient servant,

J. D. WHITNEY,
State Geologist.

LETTER OF THE STATE GEOLOGIST

RELATIVE TO THE PROGRESS OF THE

STATE GEOLOGICAL SURVEY

DURING THE YEARS 1866-7.

D. W. GELWICKS.........STATE PRINTER.

REPORT.

SAN FRANCISCO, November 25th, 1867.

To His Excellency,
FRED'K F. Low,
Governor of California:

SIR :—The geological survey of this State has been carried on during the past two years under authority of the Legislature, approved by yourself April fourth, eighteen hundred and sixty-four. Consequently, the office of State Geologist will expire, by constitutional limitation, on the fourth day of April next.

The geological survey has now been going on just seven years, as operations were commenced about December first, eighteen hundred and sixty, the State Geologist having arrived in San Francisco November fourteenth of that year. The amounts which have been appropriated by the different Legislatures for the purpose of the survey are as follows:

At the time of the passage of the original Act	$20,000 00
By the Legislature of 1860–1	15,000 00
By the Legislature of 1861–2	15,000 00
By the Legislature of 1862–3	20,000 00
By the Legislature of 1863–4 (for two years)	25,600 00
By the Legislature of 1865–6 (for two years)	30,000 00
Total	$125,600 00

Making an average of fifteen thousand nine hundred dollars a year. In my letter to yourself, dated January first, eighteen hundred and sixty-six, and published by order of the last Legislature, I gave a succinct statement of the condition of the work of the survey at that time, and I will now proceed to recapitulate, as briefly as possible, what progress has been made, both in the fieldwork and in the publication department, since the date of that letter.

I will first, however, allude to our plan of operations, as gradually developed during the progress of our work and finally brought into shape at the time of the publication of the volume devoted to geology. (See Preface, Geology of California, Vol. I., where, also, a resumé of the movements of the various parties of the survey, up to the close of the year eighteen hundred and sixty-five, is given.) According to this plan the survey is divided into three principal departments, each of which is again divided into subordinate branches.

The main divisions with the subdivisions may by seen at a glance in the annexed scheme:

A.—*Topography.*—1. Topographical Survey and Maps; 2. Physical Geography.

B.—*Geology.*—1. General Geology; 2. Palæontology; 3. Economical Geology; including Mining and Metallurgy.

C.—*Natural History.*—1. Botany; 2. Zoology.

To the above must be added the collection of a museum of geology and natural history, to illustrate the resources and geological structure of the States and Territories of the Pacific Coast.

Each one of the subdivisions specified above demands one or more volumes of the published series, for the results embraced in it. The number of volumes depends, of course, on the thoroughness with which the work is performed, and that again on the amount of money appropriated.

The following scheme shows the lowest and the highest number of volumes contemplated in each department:

Title of Work.	Lowest No. of Volumes.....	Highest No. of Volumes.....
Physical Geography..	1	1
General Geology..	2	2
Economical Geology..	1	2
Palæontology	2	3
Botany	1	2
Zoology..	3	4
Maps..	1	1
Totals.............................	11	15

Of the condition of these volumes, as regards progress in preparation for the press, information will be given further on.

The original Act authorizing the survey, provided for such a complete examination of the State and report on all departments of the geography, geology, and natural history, as is contemplated in the above synopsis of the proposed volumes; and, although the plan may to some have seemed too vast in its scope for the intelligence and the resources of the State, yet it is my firm opinion that if ever carried to completion, its suitableness will be more and more appreciated as the State increases in wealth and civilization. Had the appropriations

asked for by the State Geologist been granted, the work would, without
having been any serious burden on the people, be now far advanced
towards completion.

With the above brief suggestions, I will proceed to give, first a
synopsis of the movements of the different parties which have been in
the field during the past two years, and then a concise statement of the
present condition of our work, following the order stated above, for the
different departments.

FIELDWORK OF 1866.

1. Messrs. W. M. Gabb and F. E. Brown commenced January fourth,
eighteen hundred and sixty-six, a geological exploration of the southern
coast ranges, with the especial purpose of obtaining materials for the
palæontology of the tertiary rocks and to determine the geological
position and economical value of the bituminous materials found in Los
Angeles, Santa Barbara, and San Luis Obispo Counties. This party
reached San Luis Obispo, April eighth, and was joined by Mr. Hoffmann,
and both geological and topographical work was carried on from there
northward, in the Santa Lucia, Gavilan, and Monte Diablo ranges, until
June, when the party returned to San Francisco.

2. After writing up his notes, Mr. Gabb continued his work northward
of the Bay of San Francisco, assisted by Mr. Frank Coffee, and they
proceeded to make a detailed geological examination of a large portion
of Sonoma, Mendocino, and Humboldt Counties, returning to San Francisco about the first of November.

3. A party, consisting of Messrs. C. King, J. T. Gardner, H. N.
Bolander, and C. R. Brinley, with two men, left San Francisco, June
sixth, to commence the geological and topographical survey of the region
adjacent to the Yosemite Valley, so as to connect our work of eighteen
hundred and sixty-four, in the High Sierra, with that of Mr. Wackenrender, commenced in previous years and continued in eighteen hundred
and sixty-six and eighteen hundred and sixty-seven. The especial
object of this party was the collection of material for a map, on a large
scale, for the Yosemite Guide Book, especially authorized by the last
Legislature. (The dimensions and scale of this map will be given further on.) This party remained in the field until November first, Mr.
King carrying on the geological work, and Mr. Gardner the topographical. Both these gentlemen returned to the Eastern States in November,
where Mr. Gardner occupied himself until spring, plotting his summer's
work. These gentlemen have since been employed by the United States
War Department, by special authority of Congress, to make a geological
and topographical survey of the region bordering on the Pacific Railroad
along the fortieth parallel, in which great work they are still engaged.

4. Early in August I left San Francisco, having previously been with
the parties above mentioned for some time, to make a geographical
and geological survey of Plumas County. The party consisted, besides
myself, of Mr. Wackenrender, who had charge of the topographical
work, assisted during a part of the time by Mr. A. Hartwig, and then
by Mr. A. W. Keddie, with two men. The geological portion of the
survey I myself had in charge. This party remained in the field as long
as the season would permit, nearly finishing the work in Plumas, and at
the same time doing a part of Sierra, it having been found advisable to
combine these two counties on one map.

The above were the principal parties in the field during the season of eighteen hundred and sixty-six; but, in addition, there was considerable field and office work done, chiefly of a topographical character. Mr. Wackenrender was in the field in May and June, mapping the country between the Sonora and the Big Tree roads, across the Sierra Nevada. Mr. George H. Goddard plotted for this survey a large amount of work done in previous years at the head of the Mokelumne, Stanislaus, and American Rivers. He also plotted a considerable area along the eastern boundary of the State, including part of the White Mountain range. Mr. R. D'Heureuse commenced the survey of Kern County, on his own account, which work he was unable to finish, and which was therefore turned over to us on payment of a small portion of its cost, with the understanding that he should go on to complete it during the next year, at the expense of the survey. Mr. S. F. Peckham, in May and June, made a special detailed examination of all the important oil-bearing localities, or those which were reputed as such, for the purpose of securing a supply of material for chemical examination, and to obtain information in regard to the economical value of the bituminous substances of that region.

During the winter of eighteen hundred and sixty-six and sixty-seven, Mr. Gabb was detached from the survey, and accompanied by Mr. F. Von Löhr, made a survey of the Peninsula of Lower California, for private parties. The scientific geological results of this expedition, which were of very considerable value, as giving the first clue to the structure of an extensive and important region, were communicated to and will be published by the California Academy of Sciences.

The chemical examination of the bituminous products collected during the season was carried on at Boston and Providence during the ensuing winter, by Mr. Peckham, for the term of six months, and the results obtained by him will be embodied in the volumes of economical geology.

The fieldwork of this year (eighteen hundred and sixty-six) was prolonged until late in the season, and as early as possible the next year it was resumed, as will be seen from the following synopsis:

FIELDWORK OF 1867.

1. Mr. Hoffman, with Mr. A. D. Wilson as assistant, commenced March sixth, to work up the region of the foothills between the Chowchilla and King's Rivers. May twentieth I joined the party, and we continued the surveys to the Big Tree grant and across the Yosemite to Coulterville, where the party was broken up, Mr. Hoffman returning to San Francisco to go on with the office work. Mr. Wilson was then joined by Mr. Von Löhr, and they proceeded to make a survey of the Calaveras Grove of Big Trees on their way to the road across the Sierra, via Placerville.

2. Mr. Gabb, accompanied by Mr. R. E. Poston, about the middle of June, joined Messrs. Wilson and Löhr, and they together proceeded to the eastern border of the State for the purpose of making the necessary surveys to complete the southeastern sheet of the Central California Map. Of this party, a portion of the expenses was paid by the United States and a part by myself. Only that was charged to the State of California which was justly due for work done within its limits. This party, after exploring the White Mountain range, carried their work east as far as the one hundred and sixteenth meridian, working up the geology and topography of an extensive region very difficult to explore, and one in

regard to which there had been up to that time but little definite information obtained.

It was my intention to have the expedition extend its work as far as the eastern border of Nevada, embracing the area between the thirty-seventh and thirty-ninth parallels; but winter set in very early, so that it became necessary to leave the field during the latter part of October.

3. Mr. Hoffman, assisted by Mr. H. Craven as topographer, Mr. W. Harris as photographer, and two men, left San Francisco about the middle of August, and were occupied for about six weeks in completing the work commenced during the previous year by Messrs. King and Gardner, about the head of the Merced and on the upper portion of the Tuolumne.

They explored the interesting valley called by the Indians Hetch-Hetchy, an almost exact counterpart in its general features and in some of its details, of the Yosemite Valley. A number of photographs were taken, of which the negatives are in our possession, to be used in illustrating our future volumes in case it should be desirable. This party also made a minute survey of the bottom of the Yosemite Valley for the Commissioners, to be paid for from the fund to be appropriated for their use. This work was found to be necessary for the purposes of the Commission in carrying out the objects of the grant made by Congress to the State of California.

4. Mr. R. D'Heureuse continued his topographical work in Kern, Tulare, and Inyo Counties, with two assistants, commencing May twenty-eighth, and ending September nineteenth. This survey has been plotted on a scale of two miles to an inch, and embraces an area of about one hundred miles north and south, by fifty in the opposite direction. It takes in all the settled part of Kern County, about half of Tulare, and the western edge of Inyo, embracing the whole of the Sierra Nevada from Walker's Pass to the parallel passing along the lower end of Owen's Lake. Mr. D'Heureuse also collected a large amount of geological information in regard to the region traversed by himself. He discovered an extensive grove of the Big Trees, of the existence of which we have no previous account.

5. Mr. Wackenrender has also been engaged during the whole season, with the exception of two weeks, in continuing his surveys in the central portion of the Sierra Nevada. During this time he has made several trips along the Sierra, between Alpine and Plumas Counties, completing the high part of Alpine, Calaveras, Amador, El Dorado, and Sierra Counties. There is about three months more work to be done to enable us to plot the whole of the Sierra Nevada on the largest scale required, from Walker's Pass to Lassen's Peak, a distance of about four hundred miles in a direct line. The area of the region thus surveyed by our parties during the past four years, including only what may be called the "High Sierra," is about twenty thousand square miles, or fifty miles in width on an average, by four hundred miles long, as stated above. The counties in which the work is deficient are Tuolumne, Nevada, and Placer, but we could plot the whole of the higher portion of these with tolerable accuracy, on the six miles to an inch scale, in case of necessity.

During the past two years the State Geologist has been actively and exclusively engaged in the State attending to the necessary work of the survey in all its departments, with the exception of two short periods of absence, one of four weeks in Oregon and Washington Territory, and one of two weeks in Nevada. These excursions were made for the purpose of settling important geographical and geological questions intimately connected with our own work. Lest, however, misapprehensions should arise, I will state that for absences of this kind there is no charge made to the State, either for salary or expenses incurred.

Having in the preceding pages given a summary of our movements during the past two years, enumerating the times and specifying the localities where the principal parties were at work, I will proceed to state what progress has been made in each department, necessarily with much brevity, following the order of the scheme of our work as given above.

1. TOPOGRAPHY AND MAPS.

By far the largest amount of expenditure has been during the past two years in this department of the survey. The reasons for this were twofold. *First*—By the resignation of Professor Brewer, who left our work to take a chair in Yale College, and by the sickness and resignation of Mr. Rémond,* I had been deprived of my principal geological assistants, and the appropriation was too small to enable me to engage others without dismissing a part of the topographical staff. But the gentlemen employed in this department were engaged on work already commenced, and with which they alone were familiar; hence they could not be dismissed without entirely breaking up the topographical work, and allowing a large amount of valuable material to be utterly lost. *Second*—The want of any even approximately correct maps of any part of the State, made it entirely impossible for us to work out the detailed geology without first preparing such maps as we needed. We could neither lay down the placer mines nor the quartz veins, nor indicate the different strata cropping out on the surface, or make our descriptions of the geological structure of the country intelligible in any other than the most general way, without having an accurate geographical basis for our work. Properly, our work should be carried on *pari passu* in both the geographical and geological departments; but, if means are only provided for one, the former must have the precedence, and be completed first.

The general plan of our topographical work embraces maps on four different scales. The largest is that of a mile to two inches; this is reserved for the most important mining districts, where the special illustration of the occurrence of veins or mineral deposits makes a large scale necessary. The next is two miles to an inch; this is the scale of the Bay Map and of the County Maps in progress, as will be noticed further on. The next is six miles to an inch; this scale is adopted for the Central California Map; and finally, a scale of ten or twelve miles to an inch will have to be adopted for a general map of the State, if we ever are able to compile one from our materials. I did, in former years,

---

* Mr. Rémond left the survey early in eighteen hundred and sixty-six, being completely broken down in health—constitutional tendencies to disease of the lungs having been aggravated and hastened towards a fatal termination by his arduous exertions and devotion to the work in which he was engaged. He removed to Santiago, Chile, in the hope that the climate of that country might exercise a beneficial influence on his health. It was too late, however; the hand of death was on him, and he returned to California, after a little more than a year's absence, living only a few days after landing in San Francisco. He died at the early age of twenty-nine, May thirty-first, eighteen hundred and sixty-seven. He was an enthusiastic lover of the natural sciences, with remarkable perceptive powers, and full of energy and perseverance. Had his life been spared, he would have risen to an eminent position in his favorite departments of geology and palæontology. His valuable work in connection with our survey, and especially that carried on by him under the greatest difficulties in Northern Mexico, will entitle him to be ranked among those who have done much to aid the cause of science on the Pacific coast.

contemplate as large a scale as six miles to an inch for the general map of the State; but this would require nine sheets, and seems too extensive an undertaking for our means, or for any means that we are ever likely to be supplied with; and the publication on that scale of the Central California Map, which embraces only one third of the area of the State, but ninety-five per cent. of its population, will render it less necessary to use so large a scale for the very thinly inhabited region of the extreme north and south.

To pass to the statement of what is accomplished in collecting the materials and putting them on paper, in accordance with the above plan, the following is submitted:

(a) *Scale of a mile to two inches.*—On this scale a map of the vicinity of Monte Diablo has been completed, and is now ready for the engraver. It is two and a half by three feet in size, and embraces the most important coal deposits yet discovered in the State. It covers an area of one hundred and seventy square miles. The Map of the Yosemite Valley, made by Mr. Gardner, and engraved for the Yosemite Book, is also on this scale. It is fifteen inches by twenty-four in size.

(b) *Scale of two miles to one inch.*—On this scale the "Map of the vicinity of the Bay of San Francisco" has been drawn and engraved. This map covers an area of four thousand two hundred and forty-eight square miles of land, just about equal to that of the State of Connecticut. It is four feet by three in size, and has been engraved on two sheets. It embraces the whole of San Francisco, San Mateo, Contra Costa, Alameda, and Marin Counties, a large portion of Santa Cruz and Santa Clara, and a part of Solano, Sonoma, and Napa. This is the most densely settled portion of the State, containing as it does the heart of the agricultural and commercial region. Over one third of the population of California reside within its borders. This map has been engraved in New York, and copies of it are expected by the next steamer. Much delay in issuing it has been caused by the necessity of sending proof sheets back and forth from San Francisco to New York, and also by the numerous changes which have been made in the boundaries of ranches during the past two years.

On the same scale as the Bay Map, three maps of the central counties of the State along the Sierra Nevada, and including the principal mining region of the State, are projected. Of these, the northern one embraces Plumas and Sierra, and parts of Yuba and Butte Counties; the central, Nevada, Placer, El Dorado, Amador, and Calaveras, and portions of Yuba. Butte, Sutter, Sacramento, and San Joaquin; the southern, part of Calaveras, all of Tuolumne and Mariposa, and parts of Stanislaus, Merced, and Fresno Counties. Of these, the fieldwork for Plumas and Sierra is nearly completed, and the map can be drawn whenever the state of our funds permits it. The Central County Map is commenced, and the fieldwork about one third completed; that of the southern counties is also about one third completed. These maps are intended to show the minute details of the topography; the position of all towns, villages, mining camps, and ranches; the roads, mines, mills, and ditches; and, in short, to answer all the requirements of the different counties for geographical purposes.

On the same scale as the Bay Map is also drawn the "Map of a portion of the Sierra Nevada adjacent to the Yosemite." This is thirty inches by twenty in size, embracing between two and three thousand

2

square miles of one of the roughest and most picturesque regions of the State. It extends from Mariposa and Big Oak Flat on the west, to the head of the San Joaquin and Mono Lake on the east. It is the first accurate map of any high mountain region ever prepared in the United States. This map is now drawn, and in the hands of the engravers. It is intended to accompany the Yosemite Book.

A large amount of material in Kern, Tulare, Inyo, Alpine, and Mono Counties has been plotted on this scale, not necessarily for publication, but for use in compiling the general map of the State.

(c) *Scale of six miles to one inch.*—This is the scale adopted for the Central California Map, which embraces the region from Owen's Lake north to Lassen's Peak, and from Clear Lake east to the meridian, which passes a little east of Owen's Lake and a few miles west of Austin, Nevada. It is embraced between the parallels of 36° and 40° 30′ and the meridians of 117° 30′ and 123°. It is in four sheets, each twenty-four inches square, and covers an area of about eighty thousand square miles, of which, however, owing to the peculiar shape of the eastern boundary of California, a portion is within the State of Nevada—about eighteen thousand square miles. About one third of the area of California is embraced in this map, and as before remarked, fully ninety-five per cent. of its population, according to the last census. The four sheets are intended to be put together for use as a wall map, which will be about four feet square. Of this Central California Map, the southwest quarter, embracing the region of the coast range from about twenty miles south of Monterey to Santa Rosa, and a portion of the Sierra Nevada in Calaveras and Amador Counties, is drawn and ready for the engraver. The southeast quarter is also partly drawn, and the field work is entirely completed, with the exception of a small section east of Owen's Lake, which is not accessible without an escort. This sheet, however, will be completed so as to be ready for the engraver in the spring, making half the map done. Of the remaining half, the eastern quarter is nearly finished as to fieldwork, say four fifths completed, while the western quarter is about half done. With two parties in the field next season, this map can be completed and drawn, ready for publication, in about two years. This, the largest inland work of topography yet undertaken in the United States, as it aims to give the topography as accurately and as much in detail as it can be shown on the scale adopted, of eighty thousand square miles of country, a large part of which is very mountainous, including the highest and roughest elevations in the country, and probably on the North American Continent. The Nevada portion of the map will be filled in from various sources, among which may be particularly mentioned the Central Pacific Railroad surveys, and the work carried on in eighteen hundred and sixty-seven by the United States, both under the authority of the War and of the Interior Departments. Enough has been done this year in Nevada to give a very good idea of the topography of the western and central portion of the State, and to make the worthlessness of the maps compiled from the previously obtained data appear perfectly evident. To form an idea of the size of California and the magnitude of our work, it should be remembered that the area embraced on our Central Map is twice that of Ohio, one of the largest States east of the Mississippi.

On the same scale of six miles to an inch, we commenced at an early period in the survey a map of the coast ranges south of the Bay of Monterey, and extending to Santa Barbara. It is three feet by two and a half in dimensions, and embraces about sixteen thousand square miles of territory, in Monterey, Santa Barbara, and San Luis Obispo Counties. The information obtained from time to time during the progress of the survey has been added to it, and it is now completed as far as the fifth standard line south of the base line. A party would be able to finish the fieldwork remaining to be done on this map in two seasons, or six months of fieldwork.

(d) *Scale of ten miles to one inch.*—This will probably be the scale adopted for the final general map of the whole State, and this map would be about five feet square, in four sheets, and would also necessarily embrace a large portion of Nevada, unless the space were designedly left blank. For this map we have already a large amount of material, comprised in not less than one hundred sheets, portions of which have, of course, been used in the other maps now in progress. All these sheets should be looked on as so much plane table work, to be compiled hereafter and co-ordinated by a system of carefully conducted astronomical observations, which will fix the position of a considerable number of points on the different sheets with great accuracy. Until this is done we can never have even a tolerable map of the whole State, as there are errors and discrepancies in the work of the United States Land Office which can only be cleared up by a careful series of astronomical observations. The portions of the State where most remains to be done in the topography are the southeastern and northwestern corners, regions the most thinly inhabited of any, and where Indians have frequently been very troublesome.

2. Physical Geography.

The collection of materials in this department has gone on uninterruptedly. The number of barometrical observations for the determination of absolute heights of important points, has greatly increased during the past two years. The important investigations of Colonel R. S. Williamson in regard to the fluctuations of the barometer on this coast, are now in process of publication; and when this volume shall have been completed, it will be advisable for us to commence a systematic revision of all our barometrical works, and to publish the final connected results in a tabular form. We shall be able to give a close approximation to the heights of between one and two thousand points in this State, including all the higher mountains and most of the towns and mining camps. To compute the observations already made will, however, require not less than a year's unremitting labor; but the results will be of great practical as well as scientific value.

We have continued the investigation of other subjects connected with the physical geography of the State. Among them, the nature and distribution of the forest trees may be mentioned, as of peculiar interest.

A beginning has been made in the construction of a map on which the boundaries of the areas occupied by the principal groups of trees are laid down.

3. General Geology.

For the reasons stated above, much less progress has been made in the strictly geological than in the topographical department. Still, a very considerable amount of work has been done, as will be seen from the above synopsis of the operations and movements of the various parties during the past two years. This synopsis will also show where, when and by what persons the geological work has been executed.

A large amount of material has been accumulated for the remaining volume of geology which it is proposed to issue; but this volume will be the last one published of the series, as it will be intended as a complete resumé of all the geological and palæontological work. It will be accompanied by all the necessary sections, showing the structure of the mountain ranges, and with a geological map of California, and probably of all the Pacific States and Territories.

4. PALÆONTOLOGY.

But little exclusively palæontological work has been done within the past two years, as Mr. Gabb has been employed in the field during most of the time when in the service of the survey, as will be seen from the synopsis of the movements of our parties given above. Most of the work performed has been in the way of arranging the collection of fossils, unpacking the materials obtained, and selecting such as was wanted for description. (See further on, under the head of "Publications."

5. ECONOMICAL GEOLOGY.

It is proposed in this department to prepare first that portion of the report which includes the non-metalliferous minerals. Under this head will be included coal, all bituminous substances, asphaltum, maltha, petroleum, building materials, cements, paints, ochres, and earthy materials in general.

No plans can be made with regard to the continuation of the economical geology so as to embrace the full and complete investigation of the mines of the State, unless the Legislature can be induced to make a more liberal provision for the support of the survey. It is useless to commence in this department unless the work in it can be thoroughly done. We have enough already of crude estimates, superficial investigations, and other worthless rubbish. If properly executed, the work in this department will be of the greatest pecuniary value to the State; but the Legislature cannot expect results of this high importance without any outlay. Eminent mining engineers and chemists cannot be found willing to work with salaries less than the wages of ordinary mechanics.

6. BOTANY.

The collection of material for the botanical report has been continued during the past two years in such a manner as to be but a trifling expense to the State. Mr. Bolander has had charge of this department, and has made extensive additions to our collections and to the material placed in the hands of the botanical collaborators of the survey in the Eastern States and in Europe. Indeed, so many new discoveries have been made, that the thorough working up of our materials seems likely to occupy a somewhat longer time than was expected.

Mr. Bolander was in the field from April eleventh, eighteen hundred and sixty-six, to September twenty-fifth, collecting in Mariposa, Tuolumne, and Mono Counties. In eighteen hundred and sixty-seven he made another excursion of a month through Sonoma, Mendocino, and Humboldt Counties; and later in the season, spent some time in Santa Cruz and San Mateo. The northern part of the State, namely, Trinity, Humboldt, Klamath, and Del Norte, is the portion which now most needs botanical exploration. Another month's collecting in San Diego is also highly desirable. Professor Brewer thinks that the volume under his charge will be ready for the press during the next year.

7. ZOOLOGY.

All that has been done in this department will be found further on, under the heads of " Publications " and " Museum."

8. MUSEUM.

The same statement has this year to be repeated which has already been made so many times before. The collections of the survey are large and valuable, but are exposed to loss by fire, and are placed where there is no possibility of displaying them in a proper manner, or having them open to the general public so as to form an attractive and instructive exhibition.

But considerable has been done within the past two years towards getting our multifarious materials in order. A part of the minerals, ores, and rock specimens, are laid out on shelves, so as to be examined without difficulty. The fossils are arranged in handsome cases, and named, so far as practicable, so that they can be consulted by students in that department. The shells of the species now living on this coast have also been very carefully arranged, named, and labelled, and can be studied at all times by those interested in this branch of natural history. The plants have been placed in cases, arranged in families and genera, so far as known, and the specific names are added as fast as they are received from the various authorities engaged in working them up. The cones of all the pines, firs, and spruces, the seeds, fruits, etc., have been arranged in drawers, as well as the cryptogamic vegetation so far as it has yet been worked out.

9. PUBLICATIONS.

Since the last session of the Legislature, the following publications have been issued by the Survey:

Palæontology. Vol. II, Section 1, Part 1, comprising the first instalment of the Tertiary Invertebrate Fossils; by Mr. Gabb. This is accompanied by thirteen plates, which have been lithographed, and which will soon be ready for delivery. The text is stereotyped. It is estimated that the whole of this volume will be required for the remainder of the Cretaceous and Tertiary invertebrate fossils. A third volume will contain the other Secondary and the Palæosoic fossils, the plants, vertebrate remains, and the microscopic fossils, the material for these researches being already in the hands of eminent authorities at the East.

Geographical Catalogue of the Mollusca found west of the Rocky Mountains; by Dr. Cooper. This was prepared to facilitate the arrangement of the conchological collection and for convenience in exchanging. It contains the names and localities of eight hundred and twenty-five species, so printed that the catalogue may serve for labels as well as for a check-list.

Mining Statistics, No. 1, containing the quartz mines and mills between the Merced and Stanislaus Rivers; by A. Rémond.

In the zoological series the drawing and engraving for the volumes of birds and fishes has been going on steadily, and that of the birds is believed to be so nearly completed that the work can go to press immediately. Arrangements have also been made for editing and issuing the volume of conchology, and a beginning made on the mammals.

The Bay Map in two sheets, as mentioned above, has been in the engraver's hands for more than a year, and is supposed to be on its way out to California. It is intended to be sold separately, in various styles, and also to form one of the series in the volume of maps, sections, and illustrations.

Both maps for the Yosemite Book are drawn, and one is engraved. The illustrations are also prepared, and the work can go to press at an early day.

The finished sheet of the Central California Map will soon be sent to the engraver.

The preparation of the first volume of the Economical Geology will be commenced as soon as favorable action has been had by the Legislature on the question of the continuance of the survey.

The plan of the "Yosemite Book," in its two editions of the "Guide Book" and "Gift Book," will be found stated at length in the report of the Yosemite Commissioners. It is intended that the "Gift Book" shall be as elegant a volume as has ever been published in this country.

10. ACCOUNTS AND EXPENDITURES.

The accounts of the survey, and a complete statement of all expenditures in the different departments, will be submitted at an early date to the committee of the Legislature to which the subject of the geological survey may be referred.

It may be stated, however, that our expenditures have overrun the appropriation made for the survey. At the end of the current year I shall have expended about eight thousand five hundred dollars more than the total appropriation, as will be seen from the following concise statement:

STATEMENT OF EXPENDITURES OF GEOLOGICAL SURVEY.

To December 31, 1865,* as per account previously rendered.	$89,998 71
January 1 to December 31, 1866	22,617 66
January 1 to September 30, 1867.	15,853 40
Estimate October 1 to December 31, 1867	5,600 00
	$134,069 77
Total appropriations	125,600 00
Deficiency at end of 1867	$8,469 77

Allowing that all the fieldwork is discontinued, and nothing done for the next six months except to plot and write up the work already on hand, it will require at least six thousand five hundred dollars to continue the survey to the end of the current fiscal year, and I have to ask,

*See Report of the Committee on Mines and Mining in the Assembly to the last Legislature, in which our expenditures are tabulated in full to December thirty-first, eighteen hundred and sixty-five.

therefore, that an appropriation for the continuance of the survey during the present fiscal year, of at least fifteen thousand dollars, be inserted in the deficiency bill, or else acted on separately near the beginning of the session. Should this not be passed, it will be my duty to dismiss all my assistants and to discontinue the survey at once, a step which I should greatly regret having to take, as there is much valuable matter in my hands either in process of publication or nearly ready to go to the printer and engraver.

I might have discontinued the survey at the time the appropriation was exhausted; but I preferred to take the risk of overrunning the appropriation rather than abandon the work, although it has not been without difficulty that I have continued it, and not without considerable pecuniary embarrassment.

I have the honor to be, with high respect,

Your obedient servant,

J. D. WHITNEY,
State Geologist.

REPORT

OF THE

COMMISSIONERS TO MANAGE

THE

YOSEMITE VALLEY

AND THE

𝕸𝖆𝖗𝖎𝖕𝖔𝖘𝖆 𝕭𝖎𝖌 𝕿𝖗𝖊𝖊 𝕲𝖗𝖔𝖛𝖊,

For the Years 1866-7.

———————

SAN FRANCISCO:

TOWNE AND BACON.

1868.

REPORT.

To His Excellency, F. F. Low,

Governor of California:

Sir—As required by law, the "Commissioners to Manage the Yosemite Valley and Mariposa Big Tree Grove" beg leave to submit the following report:

The Senate and House of Representatives of the United States, by an Act approved June 30, 1864, granted to the State of California, on certain stipulated conditions, the Yosemite Valley and the Mariposa Grove of Big Trees ; and, by an Act of its Legislature, the State accepted the same and pledged itself to the fulfillment of these conditions. In the language of the Act of Congress, the grant was accepted "on the express conditions that the premises shall be held for public use, resort and recreation, and shall be inalienable for all time." It was also stipulated by Congress that the management of the premises thus granted should be in the hands of nine Commissioners, of whom the Governor of the State should be one, and who should also have the power to fill vacancies in the Board caused either by death, removal or resignation. To the Governor was also confided by Congress the power of appointing his eight associates, the first Commissioners, and this was done by Executive proclamation, dated September 28, 1864. The Commissioners first appointed were F. Law Olmsted, J. D. Whitney, William Ashburner, I. W. Raymond, E. S. Holden, Alexander Deering, George W. Coulter and Galen Clark, all of whom continue in office, with the exception of Mr. Olmsted, who has returned to the East and resigned his place, which has been filled by the appointment of Henry W. Cleaveland of San Francisco.

The surveys necessary to establish the boundaries of the grants in question, as required by the Act of Congress, were duly made in the autumn of 1864, by King and Gardner, their notes filed in the office of the United States Surveyor-General of California, and the official plat of the same has been forwarded to Washington and accepted by the Commissioner of the General Land Office, and this plat is, in the language of the Act of Congress, the evidence of the locus, extent and limits of the grants of the Valley and the Grove. A map of the Yosemite Valley was drawn by Mr. Gardner, on a scale of two inches to one mile, showing the boundaries of the Yosemite Valley grant and the topography of its immediate vicinity. This map is now in the archives of the Commission, and has been loaned by them to the Geological Survey to be engraved for use in the publication authorized by the Legislature, of which some account will be given further on in this report. For the payment of King and Gardner, for the surveys necessary to establish the boundaries of the grant, an appropriation was made by the last Legislature.

At the first meeting of the Legislature of California after the passage of the Act of Congress making the grant to the State of the Yosemite Valley and Big Tree Grove, an Act was passed accepting the grant on the stipulated conditions, confirming the appointment of the Commissioners, organizing them into a body for legal purposes and empowering them to make regulations and by-laws for their own government. The Act of the Legislature also contained provisions making it a penal offense to commit depredations on the premises, and other sections in regard to further surveys in and about the Valley and the Grove. It also appropriated $2,000 for carrying out the purposes of the Act, authorizing the appointment of a Guardian, whose salary should not exceed $500 per annum.

Soon after the passage of the Act of the Legislature accepting the grant, and providing for the organization of the Commissioners, they met, at the call of the Governor, and organized themselves by the appointment of a President, Vice-President, Secretary, and Treasurer, and an Executive Committee. They also adopted a set of by-laws for their own government, a copy of which is attached to this report. Copies of all the other official documents cited above will also be found printed with the by-laws for convenient reference. The Commissioners furthermore appointed one of their number, Galen Clark, residing at Clark's ranch, near the Big Tree Grove, guardian of the grove and valley, fixing his salary at the maximum allowed by law, namely, $500 per annum.

As by far the largest amount of work done in and about the valley, in consequence of the Act of the Legislature, has been executed by the Geological Surveying Corps, reference will first be made to this branch of the subject.

By Section 5 of the Act of the Legislature accepting the grant of Congress, the State Geologist was authorized to make further explorations on the grants and in the adjacent region of the Sierra Nevada, for the purpose of preparing a full description of the country, with maps and illustrations, to be published and sold as other works issued by the Geological Survey are, namely, for the benefit of the Common School Fund of the State.

As early in ~~1865~~ as the season would permit, a party was organized 18, by the State Geologist for the purpose of making a detailed geographical and geological survey of the region of the high Sierra adjacent to the Yosemite Valley. This party consisted of C. King, J. T. Gardner, H. N. Bolander, and C. R. Brinley, with two men employed to pack and cook. They commenced work early in June, and continued in the field until the latter end of October, being accompanied by the State Geologist during a portion of the time. Owing to unavoidable causes, this party was obliged to return from the field before the work was completed. But enough had been done to enable Mr. Gardner to commence and partly finish a map, and the following plan of publication was determined on by the State Geologist.

The work will consist of text, maps, and photographic and other illustrations, and two editions will be issued—one without photographs, the other with them. One will be called the "Yosemite Guide Book," the other the "Yosemite Gift Book." The Guide Book will contain the text of the Gift Book and the same maps, but the photographic illustrations will be omitted. The text will be such as will be suitable for a complete and thorough guide, or hand-book, to the Valley and its surroundings, including the high Sierra, and, in general, the region between Mariposa and Big Oak Flat on the west, and the head of the San Joaquin and Mono Lake on the east. The map of the region thus designated is drawn on a scale of two miles to one inch, and is thirty inches by twenty in size. It contains all the minute details of the topography of one of the most elevated and roughest portions of the State, and is the first accurate map of any high mountain region ever prepared in the United States.

The surveys for the completion of this map were continued during the months of August and September of the present year, by a party of the Geological Survey, in charge of C. F. Hoffmann, and the work is now complete, and the map ready for the engravers. The photographic illustrations, twenty-four in number, made by C. E. Watkins, with the Dallmeyer lens of the Survey, are also all printed and delivered, and the work can be put to press as soon as the State Geologist has time to attend to it. It is believed that it will be one of the most elegant books ever issued from an American press, and that it will have no little influence in drawing attention to the stupendous scenery of the Yosemite and its vicinity.

Mr. Hoffmann and party also made a careful survey of the bottom of the valley, including all the land within the talus or débris fallen from the walls, and this work has been plotted on a scale of ten chains to one inch, making a map fifty inches by thirty in size, with the number of acres in each tract of meadow, timber and fern land designated upon it, and also the boundaries of the claims of the settlers in the valley, and the number of acres inclosed and claimed by them. This map was found to be necessary for the purposes of the Commission, and an appropriation will be asked for to pay the expense of the survey and of preparing the map.

The principal grove of trees in the Big Tree Grant has also been carefully surveyed by the State Geologist, assisted by Hoffmann, each tree of over one foot in diameter measured, and the height of a number of them accurately determined. There are in the main grove, of trees over one foot in diameter (that is, of the Big Trees or *Sequoia gigantea*), just three hundred and sixty-five, besides a great number of smaller ones. The trees thus measured have been plotted and numbered, so that their exact position and size relative to each other can be seen at a glance.

The Commissioners, seconded by the Geological Survey, have thus done all that is for the present requisite toward obtaining all the necessary statistical data in regard to the valley and grove, and for making this information public in an attractive form. It may be added that the Yosemite Guide-book and the Yosemite Gift-book will both be sold, as are other publications of the survey, and the proceeds paid into the treasury of State, for the benefit of the Common School Fund.

One of the important duties of the Commissioners is the care of the valley and grove, so as to secure them and their surroundings from devastation by fire, and from wanton injury by cutting down trees and defacing natural objects. The care of the Guardian has prevented fires from running in the Big Tree Grove, and to a considerable extent has protected the Valley from wanton injury. There have been instances, however, of the felling or mutilation of conspicuous and beautiful trees, which instances were not discovered until after the offenders had left the valley and were far away from the place where the mischief was done. It is considered necessary by the Commissioners that there should be a Guardian and sub-Guardian, one or the other—during the season of visitors at least—always in or about the Valley and Big Tree Grove, in order to bring about entire safety and security that wanton damages will not be inflicted. It is also necessary that the Guardian and sub-Guardian should be endowed by the State with police or constabulary authority, so that offenders may be arrested on the spot where the mischief is • done, as otherwise it will be entirely impossible for the Commissioners to answer for the safety of the property committed to their charge. The localities are so distant from the county-seat or residence of a magistrate, that it would be impossible for the Guardian, unless this change is made, to obtain a warrant for the arrest of the offenders and get back to the place where the offense was committed, until long after the offenders had left the valley.

Aside from wanton trespassers in the valley, there are other persons residing there to whose cases we will now direct attention. And, in order to understand the position of the parties in question, it will be necessary to go back and make a brief statement of the history of the discovery and settlement of the valley, which we will now proceed to do, relying on information furnished by persons who have been acquainted with the region since it was first explored by white men.

The Yosemite Valley was first discovered and entered by white men in March, 1852, and by a party commanded by Captain John Boling; this party was in pursuit of Indians, for the purpose of taking them to the Reservation on the Fresno. During the same year a party of miners came into the valley and were attacked by the Indians, and two of the whites killed. They were buried near the Bridal Veil Meadow. Some persons connected with Captain Boling's party communicated to the newspapers an account of the wonders of the valley, and especially of the Yosemite Fall, which was described as being " more than a thousand feet high." This notice meeting the eye of J. M. Hutchings, at that time engaged in collecting materials for the *California Magazine*, to illustrate the scenery of this State, he collected a party and made the first regular tourist's visit to the valley in the summer of 1855. This party was followed the same year by another from Mariposa, consisting of sixteen or eighteen persons. The next year (1856) the regular travel commenced, and the trail on the Mariposa side of the valley, from

White & Hatch's, was opened by Mann Brothers, at a cost of about $700. This trail was purchased in 1859 by the citizens of Mariposa County and made free. The sum paid was $200.

The first house was built in the Yosemite Valley, nearly opposite the Yosemite Fall, in the autumn of 1856; this is still standing, and has been usually known as the Lower Hotel. At the locality about half a mile farther up the valley, and now known as "Hutchings's Yosemite Hotel," a canvass house was built by G. A. Hite, in the spring of 1857, and in the spring of the next year the present house was built by Hite & Beardsley. They kept it as a public house that season, and it afterwards passed into the hands of Sullivan & Cashman, for debt. It was kept 1859–61 by Peck, then by Longhurst, and from 1864 by Hutchings, who came to the valley in the spring of that year, having purchased, or made arrangements to purchase, the house of Sullivan & Cashman. The claim, however, as far as the land is concerned, is supposed to have been the property of Hite & Beardsley, at least as much their property as a claim of that kind on unsurveyed land, and in that residence, could be that of any person. In the spring of 1857, Cunningham & Beardsley had a storehouse and shop a little above the present Hutchings' Hotel. The lower hotel was kept by John Neal in 1857, and by Cunningham from 1858 to 1861. In 1862–3 it was not occupied except by occasional stragglers. For the past three or four years it has been occupied by G. F. Leidig. J. C. Lamon took possession of the upper end of the valley, above Hutchings's, in 1860, and has continued to reside there since that time, being the only permanent resident in the valley prior to 1864.

At the time the Governor's proclamation was issued, namely, September 28, 1864, the persons residing in the valley and claiming rights there were J. C. Lamon and J. M. Hutchings. Ira B. Folsom also claimed to own the ferry across the Merced, and the ladders by which access is had to the summit of the Vernal Fall. There were probably other and conflicting claims to houses and land in the Valley; but, if such existed, the Commissioners have never been officially notified of them, nor would it have been in their power to recognize them, or to decide between them.

The claim of Lamon, as defined by himself and limited by his fences, occupies the upper part of the valley, at the junction of the Tenaya Fork with the main Merced River, and comprises 378.76 acres, of which about 149 acres are good meadow land, the remainder being chiefly a strong soil, covered with ferns to a consider-

---

able extent, and requiring a large amount of labor to reduce it to cultivation. Lamon has cleared and subdued about twenty acres, and planted a large number of fruit trees, and has been especially successful in raising berries of several kinds—especially strawberries, raspberries, and blackberries—which have found a ready market in the valley among the visitors. There is no question that Lamon would have had a clear claim as a preëmptionist under the United States laws, had this been ordinary surveyed land, or provided he had remained upon it until it was surveyed and sold, supposing it to have followed the usual course of United States surveyed lands. In view of the position of Lamon's claim, which is so situated that his buildings are not at all conspicuous in the valley, and of the useful character of the work done by him, the Commissioners did not hesitate in offering him the greatest privilege it was in their power to grant, namely—a lease of his premises for the term of ten years, at the nominal rent of $1 per annum.

Hutchings's improvements consist of a small log house and a large barn and shed, with a garden and orchard, on the north side of the Merced, as well as the hotel on the south side, said to have been purchased of Sullivan & Cashman. Hutchings has resided permanently in the valley since the spring of 1864, but most of, if not all his improvements have been made since the Governor's proclamation was issued taking possession of the valley in the name of the State. It is fair to say, however, that Hutchings's improvements have been made with an eye to the preservation of the beauty of the valley unimpaired, so far as was consistent with his ideas of the amount of stock necessary to be kept for the use of the hotel. Hutchings's claim embraces 118.63 acres, chiefly of the best meadow land, and the best, or one of the best, sites for building in the valley. Considering the fact of Hutchings's long residence in this place, and of his evident desire to effect his improvements without injury to the picturesque appearance of his surroundings, and taking into view the small number of persons who up to this time have visited the Yosemite — so that keeping a public house has not been nor is likely for some time to be a matter of profit,* the Commissioners were dis-

---

* The largest number of visitors to the Yosemite was in 1866, when probably between six hundred and seven hundred persons were there, the number having been nearly double that of the previous year. In 1867 there were probably not more than four hundred and fifty persons in the valley. These numbers include persons camping as well as those stopping at the hotels. The causes of the smaller number of visitors during this year are supposed to be—first, the late-

posed to be as liberal to him as the powers intrusted to them would permit. They therefore offered him a lease for ten years of 160 acres of land, including the hotel and house, at a nominal rent. Hutchings, however, believing that he has a legal claim to a fee simple of the land occupied by himself, refused to accept a lease or to acknowledge the authority of the Commissioners, as did also Lamon. There has been, therefore, no alternative for the Commissioners, and they have commenced legal proceedings against both these gentlemen as trespassers, with the view of having the question decided (about which there seems to be no reasonable doubt) whether the State really is the proprietor of the grant made by Congress, or, in short, whether the United States have authority to dispose of the unsurveyed and unsold public land. It is not the desire of the Commissioners to put Lamon and Hutchings to any greater expense than is absolutely necessary to establish the validity of the claim of the State, and they regret that the necessity for legal action should have arisen.

The claim of Folsom to the ferry and ladders will be noticed, after speaking of the improvements made in the valley by the Commissioners, from the funds appropriated by the last Legislature. And this leads us to consider next the approaches to the Yosemite and the Big Trees, the trails and roads leading to the grants, and the facilities for visiting these places.

The Yosemite Valley is situated nearly due east from San Francisco, and distant in a direct line about 155 miles, but by the route usually traveled—*via* Stockton—it is about 260 miles. The main Merced River runs through the Valley, and access to it is therefore possible from both sides of the river. Not, however, by following up the river itself, as would naturally be supposed. This would be extremely difficult, if not impossible, as the river runs, for many miles below the Yosemite, through a narrow cañon with precipitous walls. To enter the Valley, therefore, it is necessary to rise fully 3,000 feet above it, and then to descend again, a practicable trail having been constructed from the north and south down its precipitous sides at the lower end. On the north side, the traveller may start from Big Oak Flat, or Coulterville, the latter being of late years the point usually selected.

---

ness of the season, the snow not having left the trail until late in June; second, the fact that nearly all the pleasure travel of the country has been attracted to Paris by the Exposition; and lastly, the general stagnation of business at the East.

Although there is a waggon-road from Coulterville as far as Black's seventeen miles, travellers generally start from the first-named place on horseback, ride seventeen miles, and stop at Black's over night, and the next day ride into the Valley, the total distance being forty-nine miles, of which seventeen are made the first day and thirty-two the second. The hotels in the Valley being both on the south side of the Merced, travellers arriving from Coulterville, until recently, had to cross by a ferry after descending into the Valley, as it is only rarely, and then very late in the season, that the river can be forded. This, the ferry noticed above, is claimed by Mr. Folsom, and is situated three-quarters of a mile below the lower hotel. It is possible, however, to ride up the Valley on the north side of the river, and cross at a bridge directly opposite Hutchings's hotel ; but a portion of the trail is apt to be boggy and another part is very rocky, there being much the best ground for a road on the other side. To avoid the delay of the ferry, therefore, and to make it possible for visitors to ride entirely around the Valley, the Commissioners have had a substantial bridge erected at the foot of the Bridal Veil Meadow, not far from the place where the trail descends from the north. This will enable travellers to make the tour of the Valley, after the trail on the north side has been put in good order, and early in the season, when that side is boggy, to avoid inconvenience, and also to avoid the delay and expense of the ferry.

The Commissioners have also expended a small amount on the improvement of the trail from the Valley up the cañon of the Merced to the Vernal Fall, so that visitors can ride nearly to the foot of this fall, thus rendering a visit to this interesting portion of the Yosemite much easier than it has formerly been. They have also placed a bridge across the river above the Vernal Fall, making the trip to the summit of the Nevada Fall a matter of no great difficulty, this having been an extremely long and fatiguing trip before the bridge was built. The same bridge gives access to new and admirable views of the Nevada Fall and also to Mount Broderick, or the Cap of Liberty, and is, on the whole, a quite important addition to the convenience of travellers.

The building of the bridge at the lower end of the Valley does away with the necessity for a ferry, and the convenience of the public requires that a set of steps, or staircase, shall be erected at the Vernal Fall, in place of the present ladders, which are awkward ; and perhaps even dangerous, for ladies to climb. The Commissioners propose, therefore, next year, to place a convenient and commodious staircase near the present ladders, leading by an easy and safe ascent to the top of the fall.

Since the Valley came into the hands of the State but little has been done to improve the means of access to it from either the Coulterville or the Mariposa side. From Mariposa there is a waggon-road as far as White & Hatch's, and indeed some two miles farther, but persons usually take horses at Bear Valley or Mariposa. Last season, however, arrangements were made so that travellers could be driven to White & Hatch's, riding from there to Clark's the same day, if desired; the trail between these two last mentioned places is very good, so that it is not difficult for moderately good riders to make the trip from Mariposa to the Yosemite in two days, or in three, if one day be allowed for visiting the Big Trees, four miles from Clark's ranch.

The best method, undoubtedly, to see the Yosemite Valley and the Big Tree Grove, is for the traveller to make the round trip, starting from Coulterville and returning to Mariposa, or *vice versa*. The accommodations are good at Black's, on the Coulterville side, and at Clark's, on the other side, and these are the usual stopping places on the way in and out of the Valley. But as Black's is only seventeen miles from Coulterville, the distance is quite unequally divided on that side by the Half-way House, so that one day's ride is quite fatiguing, being about thirty-two miles. This may be avoided, however, by establishing a public house at Deer Flat and straightening the road, which now is extremely circuitous, the distance from Coulterville to Deer Flat being only a little over twelve miles in a direct line, while it is nearly double that by the present trail.

The trail on the Coulterville side passes the Bower Cave, a curiosity well worth seeing; while on the Mariposa side the views from the trail descending into the Valley are sublime, and such as cannot be obtained from any other points. It is for the traveller to decide whether he prefers getting these grand general views of the Valley after he has already been there, or on his way into it. If he wishes to have the whole grandeur of the Yosemite revealed to him at once, he will enter the Valley on the Mariposa side; if, on the other hand, he prefers to see the various points in succession, one after another, and then finally, as he leaves the Valley, to have these glorious general views as a kind of summing up of the whole, he will enter by the Coulterville and depart by the Mariposa side. In that case much the hardest day's work will be the second, or the ride from Black's into the Valley.

66

A waggon-road can be made without much difficulty from Black's to the edge of the Valley; but to construct one into the Valley, down the cliffs on that side, would be extremely difficult and expensive, if indeed possible at all. On the south side a waggon-road can be made into the Valley, but the expense would be very considerable— probably not less than $30,000. A considerable saving of time and labor, for those not accustomed to riding horseback, could be made by continuing the waggon-road from White & Hatch's to Clark's, which could, probably, be done in good shape, for about $10,000.

The Commissioners do not, however, consider it any part of their duty to improve the approaches to the Valley or Big Trees. This may safely be left to the competition of the counties, towns and individuals interested in securing the travel. A small expenditure on either side will bring the Yosemite to within one day's easy ride on horseback—that is to say, easy for persons somewhat accustomed to mountain travel. And when a waggon-road shall have been extended from Coulterville to the brow of the Valley on that side, and to Clark's on the other, the trip need no longer be one which will over-fatigue travellers in ordinary health, provided they do not attempt to make the journey in the smallest possible number of days, thus sacrificing everything to the single idea of getting through the journey rapidly.

In the Valley, the Commissioners are desirous of continuing the work begun by them, of making all the most interesting points as accessible as possible, and of removing all obstacles to free circulation. The road around the Valley requires improving; the trail to the Vernal Fall needs some additional work to make it secure; a bridge must be built over the Illiluette fork, and a stair-case up the Vernal Fall. A bridge across the Merced at the upper end of the Valley, and one across the Tenaya Fork, are also desirable, and the Commissioners recommend an appropriation of $1,200 to enable them to effect these improvements during the next two years.

The following is a summary of the above report:

1. The Commissioners propose to leave the improvement of the roads to the Big Trees and the Yosemite Valley to parties interested in increasing the amount of travel on either of the rival routes.

2. They desire to continue, on a moderate scale, the improvements in and about the Valley itself, for the purpose of rendering interesting points more accessible, and to remove all charges on visitors for trails, bridges, ladders, ferries, etc. For this purpose they

ask an appropriation of $1,200, or $600 for each of the next two years.

3. They propose to increase the salary of the Guardian so that he may pay an Assistant Guardian, and in order that one or the other of them may remain permanently in the Valley during the season of visitors. For this they ask authority and an appropriation of $2,000, or $1,000 per annum.

4. They also ask for $800 to pay the necessary expenses incurred by them in preparing a plat and survey of the claims in the Valley, which has been found indispensable.

5. They intend to continue the legal investigation of the claims of the settlers in the Valley until the highest Court of law has decided on their value.

6. They leave it to the Legislature to say whether any remuneration shall be made to the settlers, Lamon and Hutchings, for damages done them by the action of Congress and the State in taking possession of the Valley.

7. They ask that police authority be given to the Guardian and sub-Guardian of the Yosemite Valley, so that offenders may be arrested at once, without the necessity of taking out a warrant at a place sixty miles distant from the spot where the offense was committed.

8. They ask for $1,000 to pay the necessary travelling expenses of the Commissioners and all other incidental expenses during the next two years.

Summary of appropriations asked for: For surveys of claims and plot of Valley, $800; for improvements in Valley, $1,200; for pay of Guardian and assistant, $2,000; for travelling and incidental expenses, $1,000: total, $5,000. The above is the smallest sum with which the business of the Commission can be carried on for the next two years.

The above is respectfully submitted, by order of the Board, together with the Treasurer's account of expenditures, as required by law.

J. D. WHITNEY,
Chairman of Executive Committee.

SAN FRANCISCO, November 14, 1867.